Men-at-Arms • 477

Macedonian Armies after Alexander 323–168 BC

Nicholas Sekunda • Illustrated by Peter Dennis

Series editor Martin Windrow

First published in Great Britain in 2012 by Osprey Publishing, Midland House, West Way, Botley, Oxford, OX2 0PH, UK 44-02 23rd Street, Suite 219, Long Island City, NY 11101, USA E-mail: info@ospreypublishing.com OSPREY PUBLISHING IS PART OF THE OSPREY GROUP

A CIP catalogue record for this book is available from the British Library

Print ISBN: 978 1 84908 714 8
PDF ebook ISBN: 978 1 84908 714 8
ePub ebook ISBN: 978 1 78200 322 9

Editor: Martin Windrow
Index by Alan Thatcher
Typeset in Helvetica Neue and ITC New Baskerville
Originated by PDQ Media, Bungay, UK
Printed in China through Worldprint Ltd

12 13 14 15 16 10 9 8 7 6 5 4 3 2 1

Osprey Publishing is supporting the Woodland Trust, the UK's leading woodland conservation charity, by funding the dedication of trees.

www.ospreypublishing.com

Dedication & acknowledgements

This book is dedicated to Tadeusz Robinski for all his help, not the least material assistance, afforded during the writing of this book, and to his family. I would also like to thank Richard Brzezinski for help with editing the text, and Pierre Juhel, who knows more about the subject than I.

Artist's Note

Readers may care to note that the original paintings from which the colour plates in this book were prepared are available for private sale. All reproduction copyright whatsoever is retained by the Publishers. All enquiries should be addressed to:

Peter Dennis, 'Fieldhead', The Park, Mansfield, Notts NG 18 2AT, UK or email magie.h@ntlworld.com

The Publishers regret that they can enter into no correspondence upon this matter.

MACEDONIAN ARMIES AFTER ALEXANDER 323–168 BC

THE HISTORICAL BACKGROUND

Tombstone of Nikolaos son of Hadymos, dating to c.300 BC or a little later (Hatzopoulos & Juhel (2009) 430 fig. 5). He apparently wears a Persian-style long-sleeved tunic, which is unusual so long after the death of Alexander. He has a *pilos* helmet and a muscle-cuirass with shoulder-guards, which presumably marks him out as a *hegēmon* (file-leader); he may perhaps wear greaves – note the carving at the knees. His shield is rimless, and therefore probably of Macedonian type, though without any evident decoration – this may have been painted on the stele. He carries a long spear, and the chape of his sword scabbard is just visible below his shield. (Kilkis Archeological Museum inv. no. 2314; photo M. Hatzopoulos)

I n 323 Alexander III 'the Great' died in Babylon at the age of 32, leaving as his only heir an unborn son by his wife Roxane. Also present in Babylon was Alexander's feeble-minded half-brother, Philip Arrhidaios. The army declared Arrhidaios joint ruler, as Philip III, together with Alexander's son, known later as Alexander IV. Philip Arrhidaios passed from the protection of one general to another until, in 317, he fell into the hands of Alexander's formidable mother Olympias; wishing overall power to pass to her grandson, she had this inconvenient uncle put to death. In due course Olympias and Alexander IV found themselves under the power of Kassandros, son of Antipatros, whom Alexander had left as regent in Macedonia.

Among the *Diadochoi* – the generals who shared out Alexander's former empire – the greatest rival to Kassandros in his attempts to install himself as ruler of Macedonia was Antigonos Monophthalmos ('Antigonos the One-eyed'). Antigonos had first risen to prominence in 321, when Antipatros gave him command of the army in Asia. After Antipatros died in 319, Antigonos conceived the ambition of uniting Alexander the Great's empire in his own hands. The fact that the infant Alexander IV was effectively a prisoner in Kassandros's hands served the 'legitimist' propaganda campaign of Antigonos well. To avoid further such embarrassments, Kassandros had Alexander IV put to death, together with his mother, in around 310 BC; thus ended the Argead dynasty.

The throne of Macedon was now open to claimants of non-royal blood. Antigonos and his son Demetrios determined to crush their rivals one by one. In 306 Demetrios won a resounding naval victory over Ptolemy off Salamis in Cyprus, and Antigonos and Demetrios jointly assumed the royal title. Their rivals – Kassandros in Macedon, Lysimachos in Thrace, Ptolemy in Egypt and Seleukos in Babylon – each claimed the royal title in 305, in which year Demetrios laid siege to Rhodes. The siege, though unsuccessful, was of such epic scale that it won for Demetrios the nickname of Poliorketes, 'Besieger of Cities'. However, the tide had turned, and the rivals of Antigonos and Demetrios increasingly co-operated against them. Their power was finally broken at Ipsos in Phrygia in 301, where Antigonos, now in his early 80s, fell fighting. Demetrios survived only precariously, mainly thanks to his still-powerful fleet. In 295 and 294 Demetrios lost all his possessions east of the Aegean Sea thanks to the joint efforts of Ptolemy, Seleukos and Lysimachos, and the king's fortune reached its lowest ebb.

Note: Except in cases of joint rule, overlapping dates indicate rival claimants

The Argead Dynasty

323–317 BC	Philip III Arrhidaios, jointly with
323–c.310	Alexander IV

The Antipatrid Dynasty

306–297	Kassandros
297	Philip IV
297–294	Antipatros, jointly with
297–294	Alexander

The Antigonid Dynasty

306–301	Antigonos I Monophthalmos, jointly with
306–283	Demetrios I Poliorketes; solely, from **294**
283–239	Antigonos II Gonatas
239–229	Demetrios II
229–221	Antigonos III Doson
221–179	Philip V
179–168	Perseus
149–148	Philip VI Andriskos

Kassandros died in 297 and was succeeded briefly by his elder son Philip IV, and subsequently by his two younger sons Antipatros and Alexander ruling jointly. They quarrelled, and Alexander called on Demetrios for assistance. However, Demetrios invaded Macedon, killed Alexander and in 294 assumed the throne himself, thus ending the 'Antipatrid' dynasty. Demetrios I ruled for five years before being expelled by a joint invasion by Pyrrhos of Epirus and Lysimachus of Thrace in 288. In 285 Lysimachos drove Pyrrhos out, and became sole ruler of Macedonia. Undaunted, Demetrios embarked on a foolhardy invasion of Asia in 287, relying on luck. In 285 he was eventually hunted down and captured in Cilicia by Seleukos. Placed under open arrest in a guarded palace, he gradually drank himself to death over the following two years. His remains were transported back to his son Antigonos Gonatas, who was still clinging on to the city of Demetrias, founded by his father, where Demetrios was buried with great pomp in the *agora* (marketplace).

In 281 Lysimachos was defeated and killed at Korupedion by another coalition of monarchs, leaving the northern borders of Macedon vulnerable to an invasion by marauding Galatian barbarians in 279. The Galatians were only expelled following the victory of Antigonos Gonatas at Lysimacheia in 277. Thereafter, the 'Antigonid' dynasty ruled Macedonia until the final defeat and conquest by the Romans.

In 274 Pyrrhos, back from Italy, attacked Macedon, and Antigonos lost Thessaly and Upper Macedon. Pyrrhos invaded the Peloponnese in 272 but was killed in battle at Argos. The 'Chremonidean' war began in 267; fought against Ptolemy operating from the sea, it lasted until 255. Antigonid power in Greece was exercised through permanent garrisons – 'the fetters of Greece' – installed at Demetrias, Chalkis and Akrocorinth. In 249 Antigonos' governor of Corinth, Alexander, rose in a revolt supported by Ptolemy, and in 234 Akrocorinth was permanently lost to the increasingly important Achaian League. Gonatas was succeeded by his son Demetrios II in 239.

Obverse of a bronze 'shield/ helmet' coin struck by Demetrios Poliorketes during his reign as ruler of Macedon (296–288); it shows a shield bearing a monogram in the centre formed from the initial letters of the king's name. An earlier issue of shields produced for this king had starbursts in the centre, and it is possible that shields bearing the monogram were first produced *circa* 290 for his attempted re-invasion of Asia (Numismatic Collection of the National Bank of the Republic of Macedonia).

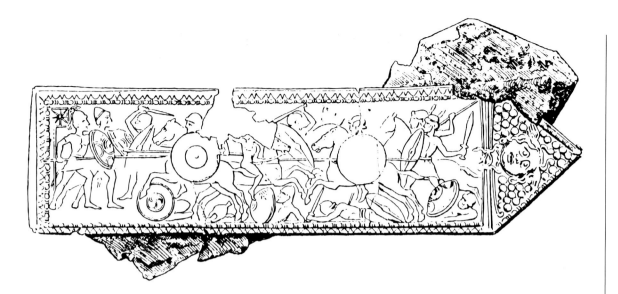

On the death of Demetrios II, Antigonos Doson (229–221) ruled as regent for Demetrios' infant son. At the beginning of his rule he repelled a Dardanian incursion, and recovered Thessaly from Aitolian invaders. In 227 an expedition to Caria followed. In 224 he led his army into the Peloponnese at the request of the Achaian League, fearful of the renewed power of Sparta under Kleomenes III. In 222 he crushed Kleomenes' army at the battle of Sellasia and occupied Sparta. Immediately recalled to repel an Illyrian invasion, he burst a blood-vessel in battle and died in 221.

The Roman wars

The new king, Philip V, was aged only 16 when Doson died. Invited into Greece by the Achaian League, he fought the Social War (220–217) against Aitolia, Sparta and Elis. Afterwards, he immediately became involved against the Romans in Illyria in the First Macedonian War. Rome's simultaneous struggle against Hannibal of Carthage absorbed most of its efforts, but an alliance with Aitolia and with Attalos of Pergamon gave Rome the advantage in Greece. After sacking the federal capital at Thermon, Philip V forced Aitolia out of the war, and the next year (205) the Peace of Phoinike was concluded. Philip then turned east, and fought a series of campaigns initially aimed at the overseas possessions of the infant Ptolemy V; but he provoked the resistance of Rhodes and of Attalos, who defeated Philip at sea off Chios in 201 BC.

Once freed from the threat of Carthage, Rome declared war against Philip in 200, and following two campaigns in Macedon and Thessaly this Second Macedonian War concluded with Philip V's defeat at Kynoskephalai (literally 'Dog's Heads') in 197. In consequence, Philip lost Thessaly, was confined to Macedon, and was forced to pay an indemnity of 1,000 talents. Philip V was a brilliant soldier and extremely popular among his men, but his constant wars had undermined Macedonian strength. The remaining years of Philip's reign were spent rebuilding it; he campaigned in the Balkans to expand Macedonian territory, founded new cities, and transplanted populations. Mines were reopened to increase revenue, finances were reformed and the issue of coinage was devolved to the cities.

Drawing of a bronze belt-plaque found during excavations at Pergamon, but now lost. The scene shows an engagement involving Macedonians using the larger variety of bronze shield, and infantry using *thureoi*. It obviously refers to a historical incident, which so far remains unidentified. On the shield at lower left, the *strovilos* symbol – a star with curved rays – suggests a 2nd-century context. Note the underarm use of the pike by the Macedonians. (After Proeva (2011) fig. 7)

Perseus succeeded his father in 179, and continued his policy of consolidation. This provoked the envy of the Pergamene Kingdom and brought on the Third Macedonian War with Rome (171–168). Perseus defeated a Roman army in Thessaly in 171, but the campaigns of 170 and 169 were stalemates, and he was finally defeated at Pydna in 168. The monarchy was abolished, and Macedonia was divided into four separate republics.

Then, in about 150 or 149, a pretender, Andriskos, claiming to be the son of Perseus, 'dropped from the skies', as Polybius put it. Raising Thracian troops, he moved into Macedonia and, by appealing to the poor, won control of the country. He styled himself Philip VI, prompting the start of the Fourth Macedonian War. The next year a Roman army under the praetor P. Juventius Thalna arrived in Greece to oust Andriskos, but it was annihilated, and Thalna himself was killed on the battlefield. In 148 the praetor Quintus Caecilius Metellus (later Macedonicus) defeated Andriskos with two legions, again at Pydna, though resistance continued for several years. Late in 148 Metellus put down another pretender claiming to be another son of Perseus, and in 143 the Romans had to deal with yet another, who raised a significant army. Macedonia finally lost its independence and became, with Illyria, a Roman province.

Roman *denarius* struck by Q. Marcius Philippus, showing Philip V wearing a cuirass with a double row of *pteruges*, and – inexplicably – his sword baldric the wrong way round, over the left shoulder. The lappets billow out behind his helmet, and below them two corners of the cloak are shown with small weights attached, so it could be of the Macedonian type. The cavalry boots are rather short, and have ornamental lappets hanging down below the laces fastened at the top. Note the large star shown on the horse's haunch, which could indicate a royal brand-mark. See reconstruction, Plate H1. Briscoe (1984) speculated that the *cognomen* Philippus went back to the siege of Rhodes in 305 BC, when Rhodes was aided by both Rome and the Macedonian leader Kassandros. The latter's son later became King Phillip IV, and the Roman Philippus may have acquired the name due to his dealings with the Macedonian crown prince. (British Museum)

HISTORICAL SOURCES

Good historical texts describing the organization and equipment of the Macedonian army exist only for the period from the 223 campaign against Kleomenes III of Sparta until the final defeat at Pydna in 168. Our main sources are the historical narratives of Polybius and Livy; the first is fragmentary, and the second has an annoying lacuna of two manuscript folios in the description of the battle of Pydna. Valuable additional details are supplied by Diodorus and Plutarch.

We have quite detailed knowledge of Antigonid infantry organization thanks to two fragments of an inscription found in the bed of the River Strymon at Amphipolis in January and April 1934; these record regulations that had been issued by a Macedonian king, almost certainly Philip V. The clauses preserved concern mounting the guard and its inspection, encampment, benefits given in kind, booty, prisoners, watchwords, and personal equipment. Hatzopoulos (2001: 144) suggests that the inscription originated shortly after 218, when resentment over the handing-over of booty nearly led to a mutiny. Another inscription that sheds much light on Antigonid military practices is the 'conscription' decree or *diagramma*, probably enacted on the eve of the battle of Kynoskephalai in 197, and reflecting the desperate conditions of that time. This is preserved in two copies, one from Kassandreia and the other from Drama; these inscriptions and others are gathered together in the epigraphic appendix published by Hatzopoulos.

Much initial work on the organization of the Antigonid army was carried out by Walbank, and more detail has been added by Hatzopoulos. To what degree this outline can be extended back for the previous hundred years is, however, questionable. The return of the Antigonids in 276, following the anarchy that accompanied the two-year Galatian presence, may have prompted a wholesale reform of Macedonian institutions.

What follows on the organization of the army is an expanded version of the present author's earlier essays, in the chapters entitled 'The Macedonian Army' in Roisman & Worthington (2010: 446–71), and 'Land Forces' in Sabin, Van Wees & Whitby (2007: 325–357); both those works contain a more detailed bibliography (see 'Further Reading', below).

ARMY STAFF

The titles 'companions' (*hetairoi*) and/or 'friends' (*philoi*) were official styles, awarded by the Macedonian kings to their closest companions. They relied on these trusted courtiers for advice on all matters, including military. However, 'companion/friend' was a court title, not a military rank, and is not to be confused with Alexander's Companion cavalry regiment. The king relied on the following institutions to run the army itself.

The 'Bodyguards'

As under Alexander, the king was further assisted in the running of the army by a select body of *sōmatophylakes*, literally 'bodyguards'. During his description of the ritual purification of the army in 182, Livy (40.6.3) states that the *agēma* marches at its head, followed by the *custodes corporis*, clearly a semantic translation of *sōmatophylakes*. *Sōmatophylakes* are mentioned twice by Diodorus (30.10.2, 11.1) during the closing stages of the Pydna campaign. At Dion one of the *sōmatophylakes* burst in on the king's bath and announced that the enemy were upon them. After the battle Perseus sent the *sōmatophylax* Andronikos to Thessaloniki to burn the fleet.

In the Alexandrine period at least, the *sōmatophylakes* seem to have carried distinctive weapons. One of the 'Royal Bodyguards', Amyntas, was brought to trial by Alexander. In an account preserved in Curtius (7.1.18) we hear that during the trial Amyntas desired to be given the attire of a Bodyguard and Alexander ordered that he should be given a lance. In his description of Flamininus' triumph in Rome, Livy (34.52.5) mentions ten silver shields, presumably badges of rank limited to a small group of senior military officers. There were originally seven, later eight *sōmatophylakes* in the Alexandrine army; their number is unknown for the later period – perhaps ten?

Hypaspists

A regiment bearing the title *hypaspistai* continued to exist after Alexander's death, but it seems unlikely that it survived for long as a formed body of troops. In the later Macedonian army the *hypaspistai* mentioned in the sources seem to have served as a lower rank of staff officers, assisting the *sōmatophylakes*. In 218, Philip V sailed from Kirrha to Sikyon accompanied by the *hypaspistai* (Polyb. 5.27.3). In the Amphipolis inscription, the quarters of the *hypaspistai* are to be put up immediately after those of the king and his immediate circle, and the *hypaspistai* can be the first to bring information to the king. After the battle of Kynoskephalai, Philip V sent one of the *hypaspistai* to Larisa to burn his state papers (Polyb. 18.33.2).

Royal Pages

The institution of the Royal Pages (*basilikoi paides*) was founded by Philip II (Arr. *Anab.* 4.13.1). Raised from the sons of the Macedonian nobility, they are described as boys (*neoi, neaniskoi*) in a number of sources (Curt. 10.5.8; Plut. *Alex.* 39.5, 49.3). They were responsible for preparing the king's bath and dinner (Diod. 17.36.5), and attended the king at his sacrifices (Val. Max. 3.3 ext. 1). They guarded him when asleep; led the horses from the grooms to the king and helped him mount (Diod. 17.76.5); and accompanied him on the chase (Arr. 4.13.1). Women could be brought to the king's bed through the royal pages (Curt. 8.6.3). One of the pages was also in control of the armoury (*hoplothēkē*) inside the royal tent (Diod. 17.79.5; Curt. 6.7.22). They would also play ball (*sphaireia*) with the king (Plut. *Al.* 39.5). These young men received a general education at court and were allowed to sit at the king's table, and only the king had the power to punish them by flogging (Curt. 8.6.2–6). They were under training to become military commanders or governors (Curt. 5.1.42).

The heir to the throne was also brought up in the company of the pages. Diodorus (19.52.4) reports that in 316 BC Kassandros took away from the infant Alexander IV the *paides* who, according to custom, were being brought up as his companions, and ordered that he should no longer receive royal treatment. The institution of the Royal Pages continued under the Antigonids. When Philip V was staying in Argos a woman was brought to his bed disguised as member of the Royal Pages – in this passage called *basilikoi neaniskoi* – wearing *krēpides* boots and a *chlamys* cloak (Plut. *Mor.* 760b). They do not seem to have accompanied Perseus to the field of Pydna, for after the battle Perseus fled to the palace at Pydna, where he was greeted by the Royal Pages (Livy 44.43.5). The Royal Pages accompanied Perseus to Samothrace, where they surrendered to the Romans (Livy 45.6.7).

CAVALRY

Clothing and equipment

The ancient Macedonians wore a distinctive type of cloak known at the time as the 'Macedonian' cloak. Semi-circular in shape, it ended in an approximately even line at the hem. Frequently the cloak was decorated with a border in a different colour. Another distinctive element of

Macedonian national dress was the *kausia*, a kind of felt beret; typically white, this was occasionally dyed 'sea-purple' when worn by important individuals or units. Plutarch records (*Eum.* 8.7) that the army empowered Eumenes to distribute sea-purple *kausiai* and cloaks, 'the most royal of gifts among the Macedonians', as kings bestow them among their 'friends'.

Boots were worn by cavalry in the ancient world. Horses's coats were generally left unshorn, and boots prevented chafing of the lower leg against coarse equine body-hair. Before stirrups were invented horses were controlled from the lower leg, not from the thigh. Infantry generally went barefoot, except in winter.

The cavalry spear in general use throughout the late Classical and Hellenistic periods was called the *xyston*, or 'whittled' spear. Its length is not given in the ancient sources, and we do not know if this varied over time. A whole class of cavalry, the *xystophoroi* or 'lancers', came into being during the Hellenistic period, named after their principal weapon.

It is generally thought that Hellenistic cavalry began to use shields only after the Galatian invasions of Greece, which began in 279 BC. These were wooden, sometimes covered in hide or felt, circular in shape, and large – over a metre (39–40in) in diameter, covering the rider from neck to thigh. They were of two main varieties. The first was reinforced in the centre by a large, circular, bronze boss (*umbo*). The second was reinforced with a smaller 'barleycorn'-shaped *umbo* set on a *spina* (reinforcing rib) across the front. The latter type only seems to have become popular in the 2nd century BC.

Recruitment

The Macedonian system under Philip II and Alexander the Great seems to have been to allocate crown lands to the *hetairoi*, each of whom in return had to furnish himself with a mount from the resources of his estate (and another for the groom who accompanied him). The mount was therefore the property of the cavalryman, not of the state. This is reflected in Arrian (*Anab.* 3.19.5), for when the allied Thessalian cavalrymen are demobilized at Ekbatana they sell their horses. If the horse was lost on campaign, however, it seems to have been the responsibility of the state to provide a remount. Curtius (7.1.15) reports that Antiphanes, the secretary (*grammateus*) of the cavalry, ordered Amyntas son of Andromenes to hand over some of his spare horses to men who had lost theirs. Alexander is known to have walked his horses when on the march rather than ridden them (Curt. 6.5.5), which would have quickly worn them out, and this was probably general practice among the cavalry.

Pompeian fresco showing the 'Embarkation of Helen' for Troy, inspired by an original series of paintings illustrating the Trojan epic commissioned from Theoros of Samos by the Antigonid court in the early 3rd century BC. The role played by the juvenile figure to the right of Helen reflects one of the duties of the Antigonid 'Royal Pages'. He is dressed in a short white cloak with a chocolate-brown tunic and open-toed *krepides*; see also illustration on page 39. Pliny (*NH* 35.40.144) states that, among other works, Theoros painted 'the Trojan War in a series of pictures now in the Porticoes of Philippus at Rome'. The Roman family of the Philippi were 'guest-friends' of Philip V of Macedon, and it is likely that the paintings found their way to Rome as gifts rather than booty. The heroes depicted in them probably represented prominent individuals at the Macedonian court. (After Ragghianti (1963) pl. 70)

Coin struck by King Antimachos III of Bactria, showing the king wearing a *kausia* with a royal diadem beneath it. The diadem was a narrow band of cloth, typically woven in purple and gold, worn by rulers as a badge of their kingship. The *kausia* was an evocative symbol of Macedonian national sentiment; in the first rounds of the wars between the Diadochoi, Plutarch states (*Eumenes* 6.1) that if the Macedonians only caught sight of Krateros's *kausia* they would go over to his side. Other depictions of the *kausia* show a deeper headband. (British Museum)

Philip II had granted estates to Companions on newly conquered land. This is confirmed by later epigraphic evidence, recording a series of grants made by the later kings Kassandros and Lysimachos. In at least one case, a grant made by King Kassandros to Perdikkas son of Koinos confirms an earlier grant made to his ancestors of estates within the territory of Olynthos during Philip II's reign (Hatzopoulos (1988) 23). So there is some evidence for the survival of this system into the Hellenistic period.

The opening lines of Philip V's 'conscription' decree preserved in the Kassandreia copy, although heavily damaged, seem to concern the inspection of cavalry horses. The ranks of cavalry commander (*hipparchos*) and secretary (*grammateus*) are both mentioned. The commander of the Macedonian cavalry at Kynoskephalai, one Leon, is called 'the *hipparchēs* of the Macedonians' by Polybius (18.22.2). This seems to be an official title for the head of the Macedonian cavalry, and is probably the same individual as mentioned in the inscription. It is probable that the *grammateus* mentioned in the inscription is the *grammeteus* of cavalry – the same position as that occupied by Antiphanes during the reign of Alexander, which institution continued into the Hellenistic period.

The 'conscription' *diagramma* probably details emergency efforts made by Philip V to expand the size of the cavalry. The inspection of horses may be the basis upon which individuals were admitted to the cavalry. The 'herald's wand' (*kerykeion*) mentioned in line 7 seems to be a reference to a brand-sign on the mouth used to distinguish mounts previously rejected for cavalry service. In line 3, 'a thousand drachmas for each horse' is mentioned. Perhaps candidates for cavalry service were paid 1,000 drachmas if the horse passed inspection: in effect the state bought the horse, the former system of service in return for land having broken down by this time.

This foot is from a bronze equestrian statue from Athens that has been identified as showing Demetrios Poliorketes, ruler of Macedon in 306–283 BC. The felt 'sock' has a split down the side to make it easier to put on, edged with a sewn-on fringed border. Note the prick-spur attached to the strap-work frame of the boot. (Athens, National Museum)

Regimental titles

Some 1,500 cavalry were left behind in Europe with Antipatros when Alexander the Great left for Asia (Diod. 17.17.5). Their nationality is unknown, but there is no compelling reason to consider them Macedonian. In 323, on the outbreak of the Lamian War, Antipatros was only able to raise 600 Macedonian cavalry, and it is clear that they were a hasty levy.

In 317, we hear of cavalry 'both those who were called *asthippoi* and those who were called "the men from the up-country settlers", being together 800 strong' (Diod. 19.29.2). It is possible that either or both of these groups had been transferred from Macedonia to the army in Asia by Antipater. Hammond (1978) saw the title *asthippoi* as deriving from *astea-hippoi*, 'city cavalry', recruited from the cities of Upper Macedonia. They may be identified with the cavalry of Upper Macedonia mentioned in 336 (Arr. *Anab.* 1.2.5). By analogy with the *asthetairoi* of the infantry, however, a derivation from *asista-hippoi*, 'closest cavalry', seems more likely (cf. Goukowsky (1987) 251–3).

After the break-up of Alexander's empire, the Companion cavalry regiment ended up as a component of the Seleucid army. The title *hetairos* continued in use in Macedonian royal correspondence, and on this basis Hatzopoulos (2001: 34) suggested that the regimental title was preserved for the elite regiment of the Macedonian cavalry. The term *hetairos*, however, could equally well be used as a purely honorific title. A dedication by *hetairoi* from Lete that is often considered Hellenistic (Hatzopoulos (1996) II, 93–4 no. 79) is in a non-military context, and could be Classical in date. Another inscription from the Perrhaibian city of Pythion records a letter sent to King Demetrios II in 234/3 by a local citizen, Philoxenos, 'from the *hetairoi* of the *chiliarchia* of Philippos' (Tziafalias & Helly (2010) 74–5); but the *chiliarchia* is an infantry formation, and Macedonian cavalry only rarely achieved a strength of 1,000 in Antigonid times.

Polybius (4.37.7) states that of the 800 Macedonian cavalry who entered the Social War in 219, about 400 were cavalry 'about the Court' (4.67.6). Polybius uses this term elsewhere (5.65.5) of the elite Ptolemaic cavalry regiment, so we cannot be sure if it is a generic term given to the 'sacred squadron' – which seems probable – or a specific title given to the elite cavalry regiment of the Macedonian army, of which the 'sacred squadron' was merely a component.

Gravestone of Nikanor son of Herakleides, dating to around 300 BC or slightly later. Nikanor wears a helmet of 'Attic' type, a Macedonian cloak, and a cuirass with shoulder-guards and groin-flaps. What has also been interpreted as a shield is more likely to be simply the rider's upper left arm. (Kilkis Archeological Museum Inv. No. 2315; photo M. Hatzopoulos)

11

The figure of the deceased from the 'Petsas Tomb' in Lefkadia, generally dated to the end of the 4th century. There is reason to identify him as a cavalry officer of an elite unit: see Plate F1 for a reconstruction of this cuirass. (After Petsas, 1966)

Livy (42.66.5) tells us that during the battle of Kallinikos the Macedonians lost 24 of their finest cavalrymen from the squadron 'which they call sacred' – *sacra ala* in Latin. Behind this lies the original Greek title *hiera ilē* (Hatzopoulos (2001) 37). Among the dead were Antimachos the squadron commander, in Latin *praefectus alae*, which clearly corresponds to the Greek *ilarchēs*. After the decisive defeat, Livy (44.42.2–3) states that Perseus set out from Pydna to Pella with the sacred squadrons (inexplicably plural) of cavalry, and that the other Macedonian squadrons (*alae*) also continued to retreat in orderly formation.

Organization and strength

It is clear from the preceding passage that the rest of the cavalry was organized into *ilai*, commanded by *ilarchai*. The strength of an *ilē* is unknown, but must have been less than 300, which is the smallest number given to any force of Macedonian cavalry (Polyb. 2.65). There was a tactical sub-unit below the *ilē*, called *turma* by Livy (42.58.6), but we lack the corresponding Greek term in Polybius – perhaps *oulamos*, the standard contemporary term for a cavalry 'troop'?

As already mentioned, 300 Macedonian cavalry took part in the Sellasia campaign of 223 (Polyb. 2.65), and 800 are attested in 219 (Polyb. 4.37.7). The cavalry force available to Philip V at Kynoskephalai numbered 2,000 (Livy 33.4.4–5), but this included the Thessalian cavalry commanded by Herakleides of Gyrton. Following this battle, the Thessalians having recovered their independence, Philip was still able to raise 500 cavalry to oppose the Dardanian invasion that followed the defeat (Livy 33.19.3).

In the army review held at Citium on the outbreak of the Third Macedonian War in 171, Perseus assembled 3,000 cavalry from all Macedonia (Livy 42.51.9); this was the highest number for the whole period for which we have good records, and was the result of Philip V's efforts to increase the recruiting base. The Macedonians were supplemented by 1,000 cavalry (and 1,000 infantry) sent by the Thracian Odrysians. The total of 4,000 cavalry is confirmed by Plutarch (*Aem.* 13.3).

At the battle of Kallinikos, fought against the Romans and their allies in Thessaly later in 171, Livy (42.58.6) states that on the left wing were the Odrysian cavalry and light infantry mixed, while on the right wing were the Macedonian cavalry with the Cretans interspersed among them. Livy (42.51.7) also sets the strength of the Cretans at about 3,000. Midon of Beroea was in command of the latter force, Menon of Antigoneia commanded the cavalry and the formation as a whole (42.58.8). Livy next confusingly states (42.58.6–9) that next to the wings were posted the royal cavalry (*regii equites*) – presumably meaning the Odrysian and Macedonian cavalry as a whole – and then came the king in the centre of the line with the sacred squadron (*sacra ala*).

In a number of successive military operations carried out during the winter of 169, Perseus first set out towards Illyria with 500 cavalry (Livy 43.18.3–4), then later against Stratos with only 300 cavalry, 'a smaller number of which he took with him because of the narrowness and roughness of the roads' (Livy 43.21.6). Later, Perseus sent 1,000 cavalry under Kreon of Antigoneia to protect the coast (Livy 44.32.6).

INFANTRY

The Macedonian pike

The pike employed by the Macedonian infantry was called a *sarisa*. According to the *Greek–English Lexicon* of Liddell & Scott the word *sarisa* was commonly written by the ancient Greeks themselves with two *sigmas* in the middle 'from ignorance that the 'i' was by nature long'. According to Noguera (1999: 849–50), the ancient Macedonians applied the word *sarisa* generically to all spears; to the Greeks, however, it specifically indicated the long pike used by the Macedonians. The most distinctive feature of the *sarisa* was its great length. The longest *sarisai* recorded in the ancient sources (Polyaen. *Strat.* 2.29.2) were 16 cubits long (7.92m = 26ft), used at the siege of Edessa by King Kleonymus of Lakedaimon, probably in 274 BC. Polybius (18.29.2) states that in his day the *sarisa* was normally 14 cubits long (6.93m = 22ft 9in), though it had originally been 16 cubits.

The ancient evidence concerning the *sarisa* has been badly interpreted in the past. The following section is based on an earlier article by the author (2001), to which readers seeking more detail are referred (see 'Select Bibliography'). A passage in Theophrastus (*HP* 3.12.1–2), relevant only to the length of the *sarisa*, has been widely misinterpreted as evidence that cornel-wood (wild cherry – *kraneia* in Greek) was used for the shaft. It reads:

Roman *denarius* struck by L. Manlius Torquatus in 113 or 112 BC, showing on the reverse a Hellenistic, perhaps Macedonian cavalryman. The cavalry shield with a reinforcing *spina* would indicate a 2nd-century date for the original image upon which this coin is based. Note the cavalry boots with lappets. The high-crowned helmet with a horsehair plume closely resembles the cavalry helmet shown in the Tomb of Lyson and Kallikles (see Plate G1). Helmets of this type were also used in other Hellenistic armies, but never, it seems, by Roman cavalrymen. Finally, note the Greek letter *rho* which appears above the figure, which compares with the *phi* that appears on some coins struck by the Philippi showing the head of Philip V. The coin type presumably refers to some event in the career of an ancestor of the moneyer, and it is worth noting that Frontinus (*Strat.* 3.5.3) mentions one A. Torquatus commanding a Roman army laying siege to a Greek city. (British Museum)

RIGHT
Macedonian cavalryman
shown on the Aemilius Paulus
Monument from Delphi, which
commemorates the Roman
victory at the battle of Pydna in
168 BC. The large round cavalry
shield with its small 'barleycorn'
umbo boss set on a *spina*
reinforcing rib is typical for the
2nd century BC. (After Kähler
(1965) pl. 18)

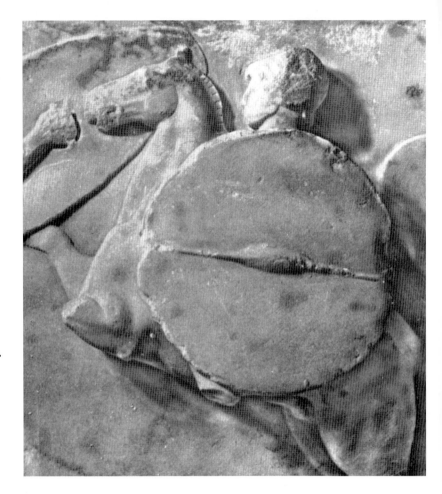

BELOW
This huge spear was excavated
and published by Andronicos.
The bronze butt is of a
distinctive type consisting of a
socket-tube, quadruple flange
and talon; it is 44.5cm (17.5in)
long and weighs 1.070kg (2.37lb).
The head is of iron, 51cm (20in)
long and weighing 1.235kg
(2.7lb). It is hard to believe
Andronicos's identification
of it as a *sarisa*, and it more
probably served as a badge of
senior rank belonging to one
of the *sōmatophylakes*. (After
Andronicos (1970) 100 fig. 9)

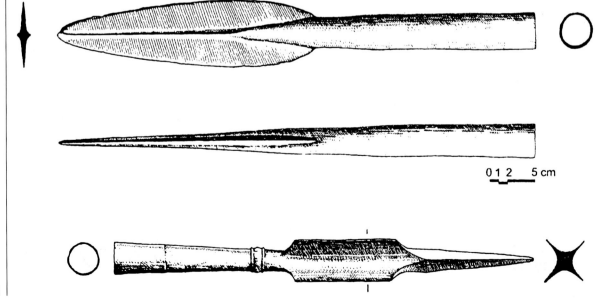

0 1 2   5 cm

The wood of the 'male' tree has no heart, but is hard throughout, like horn in closeness and strength; whereas that of the 'female' tree has heart-wood and is softer and goes into holes; wherefore it is useless for javelins. The height of the 'male' tree is at most 12 cubits, the length of the longest *sarisa*, the stem up to the point where it divides not being very tall.

A 'male' cornel-wood tree (wild cherry), from Warsaw University Botanical Gardens. The tree, as Theophrastus states, could grow to be equal in total height to the tallest *sarisai*, but its low-branching shape would make it impossible to use wood from the trunk in their manufacture. (Author's photo)

Theophrastus states that the flawed wood of the 'female' tree is useless for javelins. The implication is that only the trunk wood of the 'male' tree was generally used to manufacture javelins – and only javelins. Secondly, Theophrastus states that the height of the tree is at most (i.e., normally less than) the length of the longest *sarisa*. The *sarisa* is only mentioned to help visualize the height of the tree. Theophrastus was writing at the end of the 4th century, an age of constant warfare, and the ancient reader would have been familiar with the sight of a *sarisa*. There is no indication that the *sarisa* was actually made of cornel-wood. Theophratus's statement that only the tallest wild-cherry trees grow to the length of the tallest *sarisa* logically means that most such trees could

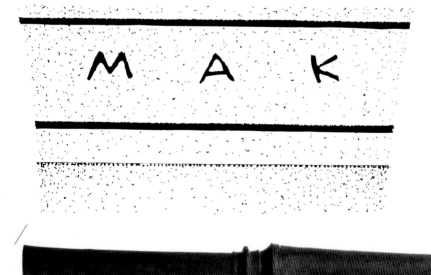

This bronze spear-butt, 38cm (14.9in) long, has traces of pitch inside to glue it to the shaft. Of unknown provenance, it is very similar in shape to the spear-butt shown in the 'Bella' Tomb. Upon cleaning off layers of corrosion in 1977, the letters 'MAK' painted in black were uncovered around the socket; this is first-rate evidence for the issue of military equipment by the Macedonian state during the Hellenistic period. On the basis of the letter-forms, a date in the late 4th century BC has been suggested. (Great North Museum, Newcastle upon Tyne)

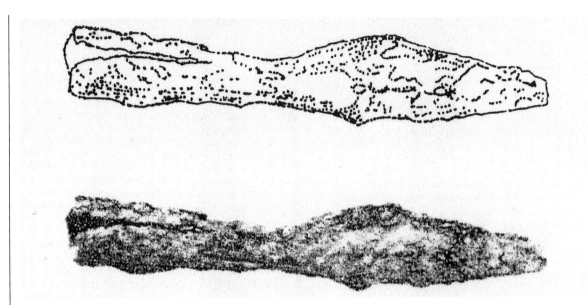

Spearhead of Robinson's Group AII (no. 2146) from Olynthus. Robinson (1941, p. 412–3, pl. cxxvii) identified this type as *sarisa* heads. They seem to be approximately the same shape as those shown on the Alexander Mosaic, but their sockets are extremely narrow, measuring 1.5cm (0.6in) at most. If the ends of the shafts were extremely tapered the identification might stand, but the possibility exists that Robinson's type AII heads may have been used to tip javelins. (Author's drawing)

not be used to manufacture that weapon. Finally, the comment that the stem or trunk of the tree is not very tall before it divides into branches clearly indicates that cornel-wood from the trunk would not be long enough to be make *sarisa* shafts.

In fact, ash was the wood used for the shaft of the *sarisa*. It has been calculated that a cornel-wood shaft measuring less than 15 feet would have weighed over 9lb (4kg), without the weight of the spear-head and butt – i.e., nearly twice the weight of an ash pike in the Early Modern period. Statius, a poet of the 1st century AD, specifically states (*Theb.* 7.269) that 'The Macedonians by custom brandish ash *sarisai*'. The quality of ash which makes it so popular for spears is its combination of strength, flexibility and lightness. Pliny (*HN* 16.84[228]) states that 'Ash is the most compliant wood in work of any kind, and is better than hazel for spears, lighter than cornel, and more pliable than service-tree (sorb)'. Other woods might be stronger, but ash was chosen for its combination of strength with light weight. This was mainly due to its straight and even grain, and any imperfections in the grain would be eradicated during the process of preparing the shaft for use.

An ash-tree with a trunk of suitable length would be felled in mid-winter, when it held the least sap. During seasoning the sap dries out of the wood, a slow process during which internal splits could develop in the trunk. These potential weaknesses in the spear-shaft were eradicated in the next stage of the process, when the trunk was split with a hammer and wedges into progressively smaller sections, until a billet of suitable thickness was obtained. The billet was then smoothed off and rounded into shape with a spoke-shave. A pike-shaft produced in this way would taper from butt to tip, with its centre of balance towards the rear. Polybius (18.29.3–4) states that the *sarisa* is held with both hands, beyond which it projects 10 cubits in front and 4 behind. Theophrastus (*HP* 3.11.3–4), writing at the very end of the 4th century, states that Macedonia was well provided with ash. It is highly probable that the production and storage of pike-shafts was regulated by the state, given the heavy demand at times that were difficult to predict.

At the final stage of production the iron pike-head was secured to the shaft with hot pitch. In his hunting manual the Augustan poet Grattius (*Cynegeticon* 117–120) recommends the prospective hunter to select a well balanced spear, and continues: 'What if I allow myself to speak of the immense pikes of the Macedonians? / How long are the shafts and how mean the teeth they spike them with!'. The head of the *sarisa* was small and made of iron, since a broad head would dissipate the penetrative force of the pike-thrust over a larger surface area. The penetrative power of the *sarisa* was attested at Pydna, where Plutarch (*Aem.* 20. 2), based on the eyewitness account of Scipio Nasica, states that the Romans were skewered on the Macedonian pikes, armour and all, 'for neither shield nor cuirass could resist the force of the *sarisa*'. Diodorus (17.84.4) mentions an incident during Alexander's campaign in India when the Macedonian phalanx was ordered to exterminate a body of Indian mercenaries who were withdrawing under the terms of a truce: 'pushing through the shields of the barbarians with their *sarisai*, the Macedonians pressed the iron heads into their lungs'.

Macedonian shields

Macedonian phalangites are recorded carrying their *sarisai* two-handed at Pydna (Plut. *Aem.* 20.2). Modern historians have long considered it impossible that the *sarisa* was wielded with both hands while the shield was being held at the same time, and they write that it would have been necessary to hang the shield from the neck by a strap. However, experimental archaeology has shown that, with practice, it is entirely possible to carry a shield effectively in conjunction with a *sarisa* of as much as 5.8m (19ft) in length (Connolly (2000) 112). The handle arrangement was different to that of the hoplite shield. In 228, Kleomenes III of Sparta armed his phalanx 'in the Macedonian manner': each man held his *sarisa* with both hands and carried his shield by an *ochane* ('handle') rather than the hoplite shield's *porpax* or handgrip (Plut. *Cleom.* 11.2).

Prior to Antigonos Gonatas's victory over the Galatians at Lysimacheia in 277 BC, he issued coins bearing a Macedonian shield emblazoned with the royal monogram formed from the letters 'ANT'. Note the cheek-guards on the *pilos* helmet shown on the other side of the coin. These 'shield/helmet' coins are sometimes attributed to the much later reign of Antigonos Doson in the 220s BC. (Drawing by Dorota Sakowicz)

Antigonos Gonatas attributed his victory at Lysimacheia to the intervention of the god Pan. In this coin the god is shown nailing Galatian arms, including long, oval *thureos* shields, to a trophy. (Kunsthistorisches Museum Wien)

Macedonian shields appeared in two sizes. This is confirmed by three bronze shields with diameters of 74cm (28.35in), 73.6cm and 66cm (26in) found on the territory of modern Greece (Pandermalis (2000) xxi), and more recent finds from Staro Bonče with diameters of 74cm, 72cm, and 66cm (Juhel, 2007). These shields were all originally inscribed with the name of Demetrios (standing for Demetrios I Poliorketes), around a starburst in the centre of the shield. This inscribed border is a detail omitted on most coins.

Asclepiodotus (*Tact.* 5.1) is describing the smaller type when he recommends 'the Macedonian bronze shield of eight palms width and not too concave'. If this type of shield measured 66cm, the Macedonian palm therefore measured about 8.25cm (Hammond, 1996), and the foot 33cm, equal to the Pergamene foot (13in) which was in general use during the Hellenistic period. Asclepiodotus is describing Macedonian *peltai*. The *peltē* was a shield smaller than the standard hoplite shield, and without its most distinctive feature – its offset rim, at least according to Aristotle (fragment 498, ed. Rose). In the Classical period, *peltai* were made of leather or wood, but in the Hellenistic period they were also made of bronze, at least *peltai* of the Macedonian type. This is confirmed by an Athenian inscription (*IG* ii² 1487, 96–7) mentioning bronze Macedonian *peltai*. The bronze plating on the outside of the larger and smaller varieties of Macedonian shields was decorated in similar style, with geometric designs within concentric bands of decoration. The smaller *peltai* tended to be decorated less elaborately than the larger variety, and in some cases they were left plain bronze. It was Reinach (1910: 444–6) who first established that the larger bronze shields, about 74cm (28.35in) in diameter, were used by the Macedonian regiment known as the *chalkaspides*, so he dubbed this shield the *chalkaspis*. Although this word is not found in any ancient text relating to Macedonian practice, his suggestion may be quite sound.

Macedonian shields are shown on Macedonian coins, allowing us to trace their iconographic evolution, at least in general outline. At first they are decorated in the centre with purely symbolic devices – e.g. thunderbolts, torches and stars, *gorgoneia*, or the heads of gods or heroes. Subsequently, monograms formed from the initial letters of the king's name begin to appear during the reigns of Demetrios Poliorketes, Pyrrhos, and Antigonos Gonatas from the 290s to 277 (and possibly also in 239–229 during the reign of Demetrius II). Next in sequence are coins showing Macedonian shields decorated with the king's portrait, often

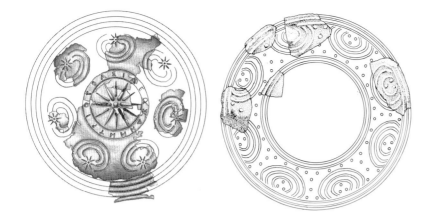

modified to incorporate attributes of the monarch's protective deity or hero. The first Macedonian king to display his portrait thus was Antigonos Gonatas, but only after 277 and his victory at Lysimacheia. Later on, Philip V appeared on coins 'heroized' with the attributes of Perseus.

The centre is surrounded with concentric bands of decoration filled with repeated geometric patterns, including crescents, *peltai*, miniature thunderbolts, balls, etc. In these bands of subsidiary decoration it is also possible to discern a chronological evolution. For example, the star with curved rays – the *strovilos* or 'whirlygig' – only appears in the 2nd century.

All six bronze examples of Macedonian shields found so far are early, dating from the reign of Demetrios Poliorketes, but there is no reason to doubt that the later shield designs, featuring royal monograms or the monarch's heroic head, reflect reality. This is to some extent supported by representations of Macedonian shields in sculpture. An inscribed stele from the Thessalian city of Gonnoi shows a shield emblazoned with the heroic head of Philip V, and there is a second similar one from Delos (Liampi (1998) 71, S25). The head of the king on a Macedonian shield, incorporating symbols of Perseus, appears on coins of Philip V, and continue on the regal coinage of his son King Perseus. However, contemporary 'civic issues' of Macedonian coins and the Aemilius Paulus Monument both show shields decorated with geometric designs in their centre, so it remains questionable whether these coins bearing the monarch's idealized portrait on a shield represent the designs used on actual Macedonian shields.

It seems, then, that shields with new blazons would be issued to the Macedonian phalanx periodically – typically, upon the accession of a new monarch, during preparations for a new war, or after a decisive event that lead to a major change in royal iconography.

Helmets

There were two fundamental changes to infantry equipment that began to appear before the death of Alexander the Great: the issue of Macedonian shields and *pilos* helmets to replace hoplite shields and 'Phrygian' helmets. The 'shield/helmet' bronze coinage issued either by Alexander himself or by his son Alexander IV shows a *pilos* helmet on one side and a Macedonian shield on the other. Juhel (2009) has drawn attention to a previously ignored passage of Sextus Julius Africanus (*Kestoi* 1.1.45–50), which states that Alexander issued Lakonian (*pilos*) helmets to his army, apparently in the latter part of his reign. In Macedonia itself, however, the 'Phrygian' helmet continued in use for some time, as attested by the frescoes of the Agios Athanassios tomb (Plates E2 & E3). In later literary contexts the *pilos* helmet seems to be referred to as a *kōnos*.

Cuirasses

The Amphipolis military regulations threaten common soldiers of the phalanx with a fine of two obols for being without a *kothybos* (a term which we do not understand fully), greaves or *kōnos*; three obols for being without a *sarisa* or sword; and a drachma – equal to 6 obols – for being without a shield. The fines for *hegēmones* (literally, 'leaders') are doubled for these items, and in addition two drachmas for being without a cuirass and a drachma for being without a half-cuirass. In Hellenistic Macedonia the term *hegēmon* had started to be applied not only to officers, but to all soldiers in the first rank. This seems to indicate that only those in the front rank were equipped with body armour.

Recruitment

Alexander's line infantry were organized into six *taxeis* each of 1,500 men, which at first were recruited on a territorial basis. When reinforcements from Macedonia reached Alexander after the battle of Gaugamela the infantry were assigned to the *taxeis* 'by tribe' (Arr. *Anab.* 3.16.11). During the reign of Alexander the infantry ceased to be allocated to units on a regional basis.

The early 2nd-century funeral stele of Zoilos, son of Ischomachos, from Marvinci – possibly the ancient Idomene. Zoilos has been identified as a peltast (Hatzopoulos (2001) 71) from the small size of shield that he carries. He wears a *pilos* or *kōnos* helmet, and a cuirass with groin-flaps that identifies him as a *hegēmon*, a warrior who fights in the front rank. (Museum of Macedonia, Skopje; photo Zbigniew Joćko)

Polybius (5.97.3–4) mentions the levies of Upper Macedonia and of Bottiaia and Amphaxitis: but he speaks of levies, and not of formed regiments. In the Hellenistic Kingdom of Macedon recruitment was based on 'the cities of Macedon' (Livy 33.3.2, 19.3). The young men of Macedonia received their military training in the cities in which they were registered. A decree dating to the early 2nd century from Beroia concerning the duties of the city's *gymnasiarchos* throws some light on these matters. The *gymnasiarchos* had to be aged between 30 and 60. Boys (*paides*) and young men (*neoi, neaniskoi*) up to the age of 30 could use the *gymnasion*, but older men had to use private facilities. The *epheboi* (normally young men in their 18th and 19th years) and those up to 22 years old had to train in throwing the javelin and in shooting the bow every day (Gauthier, Hatzopoulos 1993: 29–34).

Within the city, each household - *pyrokausis*, interpreted as 'hearth' by Hatzopoulos (2001, 91) - was liable to supply one adult male for service, as is clear from the conscription *diagramma* of Philip V. This decree, enacted under emergency conditions on the eve of Kynoskephalai, contains elaborate provisions as to who was liable for service, including 15-year-old youths if no-one more suitable was available. The sons of those deported to Rome after the fall of Macedon were also deported if aged over 15 (Livy 45.32.3), so this was, in a sense, considered an age of majority, but Philip V's decree was clearly issued in exceptional circumstances. Normally men were only conscripted on reaching their 20th year, as was the case in many Greek states. Those under this age would not normally be called upon to fight outside Macedon. The *epheboi* could, however, be called upon to fight in defence of their own land. This is probably what Livy (44.11.7) means when he describes how the young men (*iuventutes*) of Kassandreia manned the ramparts of their city.

When war came, the whole population liable for recruitment was mobilized and concentrated in one place, and only then were the various formations and units of the army constituted. For example, before the outbreak of the Social War in the spring of 219 BC, Philip V, while wintering in Macedonia, spent his time in diligently levying troops for the coming campaign (Polyb. 4.29.1). The 'best' recruits, which normally meant the wealthiest (*euporōteroi*), would go to the *agēma* and the peltasts, the less well-off to the *chalkaspides*. The newly formed army would then be ritually 'purified' by marching between the two halves of the body of a dog which had been cut in two, but the significance of this practice remains unknown.

Organization

The first fragment of the Amphipolis military regulations mentions officers called *tetrarchai*. Roussel (1934: 43) suggested that the *tetrarchia* they commanded consisted of 64 men, comprising four files each of 16 men, as in the tactical manuals written by Asklepiodotos (2.8) and Aelian (9.2). The tactical writers call the file a *lochos*, and its commander a *lochagos*.

A separate inscription from the city of Greia dating to 181 records a petition for land made to Philip V by a group of soldiers 'with Nikanor the *tetrarchēs*'. A list of names at the end of the inscription is headed by Nikanor the *tetrarchēs*, Theoxenos the *hypaspistēs*, Bilos the *lochagos*, 'and of those fighting in the first *lochos*' at least six individuals (the inscription is incomplete). Walbank (1940: 289) thought Theoxenos the *hypaspistēs* to

The *strovilos* or 'whirlygig' motif only appears on later representations of the Macedonian shield on coins. This example is a bronze coin issued by the city of Lychnidos (modern Ochrid) between 187 and 171 BC. (Numismatic Collection of the National Bank of the Republic of Macedonia)

be a member of the army staff, perhaps delegated to keep watch over the garrison stationed at Greia. As far as the mention of the 'first *lochos*' is concerned, Welles (1938: 249) supposed that the term is used in the sense of the first *lochos* or squad of the platoon commanded by the *tetrarchos* (lieutenant), the *lochos* having a war-strength of 15 men plus their *lochagos*, and that the *lochoi* in the *tetrarchia* were numbered from one to four. The *tetrarchos* would belong to the 'first' *lochos*, drawn up on the right of the *tetrarchia* in battle, both in combat and for administrative purposes.

The second fragment of the Amphipolis inscription mentions the *stratēgoi* and the *speirarchai* and the *tetrarchiai* in sequence of rank, then 'the other *hēgemones*' (all stationed in the first rank), and finally the *hypēretai* and the *archypēretai*. The *speira* is mentioned as a subdivision of the Macedonian phalanx by Plutarch (*Phil.* 9.4) and Polybius (2.66.5, cf. 5.4.9). The Macedonian word *speira* may be related to the Greek *cheir*,

This figure from the Aemilius Paulus Monument shows a 2nd-century infantryman carrying a Macedonian shield and wearing a comb-crested helmet, clearly a later and squatter version of that shown in the tomb of Lyson and Kallikles. Note the outward flare of the helmet at the back above the nape of the neck, and the volute at its termination above the cheek-piece – features it has in common with the red-painted helmet in the tomb, reconstructed in Plate G2. (After Kähler (1965) pl. 21 bottom)

23

literally 'hand', but sometimes used to mean a force of soldiers. It is regularly used to translate the semantically related Latin word *manipulus* – literally 'a handful', but used in a military sense to mean two centuries of troops. Feyel (1935: 47) suggested that the *speira* was the equivalent of the *syntagma* of 256 men, mentioned by the tactical writers, composed of four *tetrarchiai*. The *hypēretes* was a kind of 'sergeant-major' attested in other Hellenistic armies. Both Asclepiodotus (2.9) and Aelian (9.4) mention that each *syntagma* had its *hypēretes*, so Feyel (1935: 42) suggested that in the Antigonid army each *speira* had its *hypēretes*. Ptolemaic texts link the *archypēretēs* with the *stratēgos*, suggesting that each of the *stratēgiai* (groupings of the army at a higher level), each commanded by a *stratēgos*, would also have had its *archypēretēs*.

The *stratēgia* is mentioned in the first fragment, which also mentions military secretaries (*grammateis*) and then the *hypaspistai*. The *grammateis* might have been found at a higher level – we have already mentioned the *grammateus* of the cavalry. The *grammateis* were supervised by a single *archigrammateus* for the army as a whole (Plut. *Eum.* 1.2), as was also the case in the Ptolemaic and Seleucid monarchies.

The phalanx was mobilized up to a strength of 16,000 for the Kynoskephalai campaign. Interestingly, this corresponds to the 16,384 given by the ancient tactical writers as the 'ideal' strength of an ancient phalanx. Walbank (1940: 294), apparently under the influence of Feyel, proposed that four *chiliarchiai* may have been grouped into a *stratēgia*, 'an army corps of something over 4,000 men, under a *stratēgos*'. We might speculate that the phalanx at Kynoskephalai was organized into four *stratēgiai*.

The *chiliarchia*

Another level of Antigonid infantry organization, the *chiliarchia* or 'thousand', seems to have existed between the *speira* and the *stratēgia*. Feyel (1935: 54–5) noted that the *chiliarchia* is attested for the army of Alexander and by the tactical writers, and that *chiliarchoi* could be restored in the lacuna of the second fragment before *speirarchai* and *tetrarchai* at I.17, although the *stratēgoi* appear in this place in the list of officers given at I.12–3 further up. The fact that the corps of *peltastai*, for one, 'are always mentioned in thousands suggest that they were organized in chiliarchies' (Walbank (1940) 292).

A play known as the *Perikeiromenē* of Menander, written about 302–301 BC, is set in Corinth, which was then occupied by a Macedonian garrison. The military details given by Menander may therefore be relevant to the Antipatrid army. Polemon is a soldier of unknown nationality (presumably a mercenary commander) who has bought a house in the city. The slave Davus calls him 'a feather-crested' *chiliarchos* (line 174), which indicates that the rank existed in the Macedonian army at this time, and that *chiliarchoi* were distinguished by their crests.

An even clearer reference to the *chiliarchia* has recently been found in an inscription dating to 233–231 addressed to Demetrios II from Philoxenos, a citizen of the Perrhaibian city of Pythion, who was a *hetairos* serving in 'the *chiliarchia* of Philip' (Tziafalias & Helly (2010) 74). Here the *hetairos* should be understood as an honorific title and not a descriptor of regimental affiliation, since the rank of *chiliarchos* only existed in the infantry.

24

(continued on page 33)

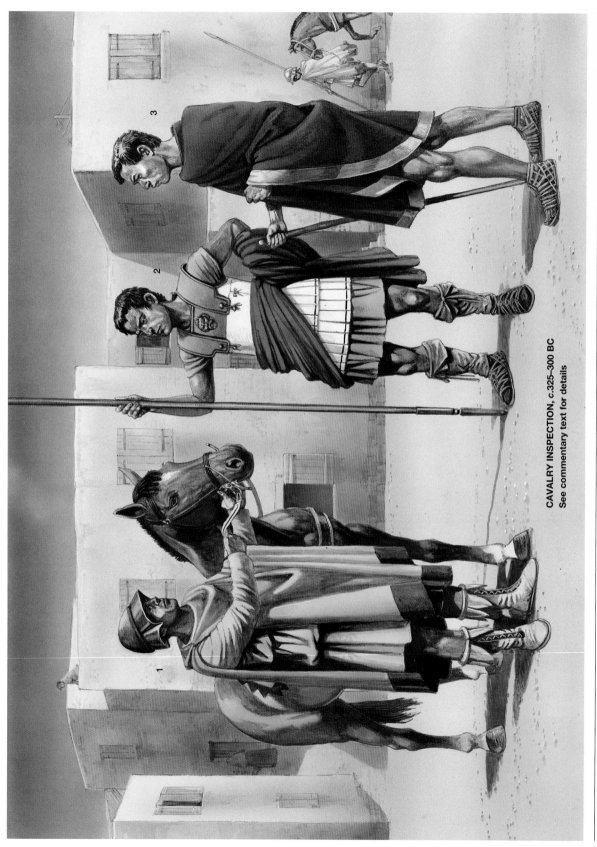

CAVALRY INSPECTION, c.325–300 BC
See commentary text for details

A

GUARD CAVALRY, c.325–300 BC
See commentary text for details

B

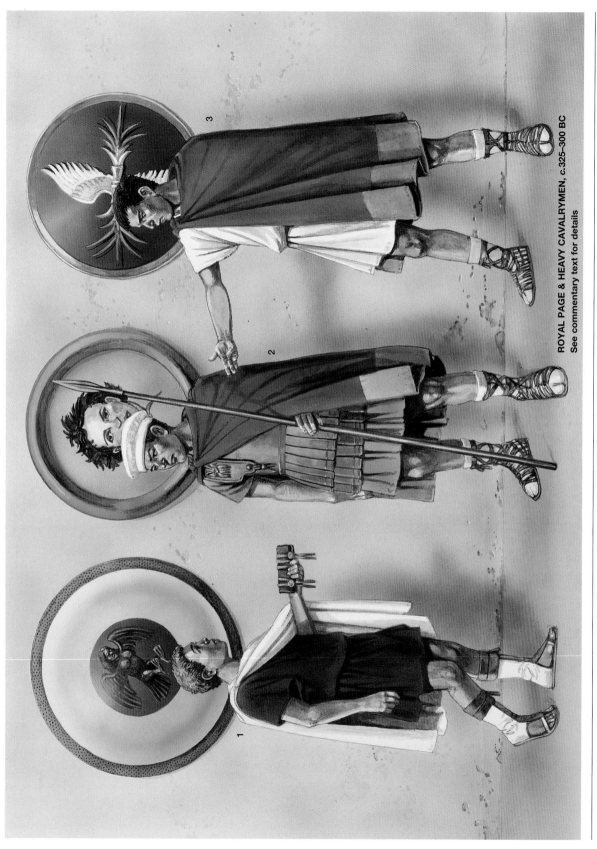

ROYAL PAGE & HEAVY CAVALRYMEN, c.325–300 BC
See commentary text for details

C

LIGHT CAVALRY, c.325–300 BC
See commentary text for details

INFANTRYMEN OF THE GUARD, c.325–300 BC
See commentary text for details

1

2

3

E

THE MACEDONIAN ARMY, c.280 BC
See commentary text for details

F

LYSON AND KALLIKLES, c.222 BC
See commentary text for details

Pay

Menander (in line 160 of his poem) mentions the military rank of '*dioikētēs* (comptroller) of the armies'. Later (in lines 261–2) he notes that Polemon is paid four drachmas a day instead of four obols, which was presumably the wage of a common soldier. The rates of pay in the Antigonid army are not known. Later still (lines 272–3), Sosias, a servant of Polemon, talks about his 'lads with *peltai*' who have been called four-obol men by Davus, and (at line 275) he threatens the latter with a *sarisa*, suggesting that they are a regiment of mercenary peltast-pikemen.

Pay in the Macedonian army was not issued regularly but only as funds became available. A key source of income, both for the king and for the common soldier, was booty. Long-standing grievances over the ownership of booty, fanned by disloyal officers, led to mutiny in 218 BC, early in the reign of Philip V (Polyb. 5.25.1–3; Juhel, 2002). In the Amphipolis regulations Philip V stipulated how booty was to be collected.

THE PHALANX REGIMENTS:

The *peltastai*

The elite regiment of infantry in the Antigonid army were called the *peltastai*. As the name implies, they were equipped in the same way in which Philip II had equipped his phalanx, with the *peltē*, the smaller variety of Macedonian shield. When Livy translates Polybius's Greek he calls them *caetrati*, an Iberian term more familiar to his Roman readership for soldiers who employed small-sized shields.

In his description of the battle of Pydna, Plutarch (*Aem.* 19.1) mentions the peltasts bringing down the *peltai* they carried from their shoulders and putting their *sarisai* in place. Asclepiodotus (*Tact.*1.2) says that the *peltastai* used a much shorter spear than the hoplites of the phalanx, and Aelian (*Tact.* 12) stipulates that the *sarisa* ought to be no shorter than 8 cubits (12 feet). It may be, then, that the *sarisai* used by the *peltastai* measured only 8 cubits. Later on, Plutarch (*Aem.* 20.5) emphasizes the diminutive size of the weapons they carried by calling their swords 'small *encheiridia*' and their shields '*peltarioi*'. In Flamininus' triumph in Rome following his victory at Kynoskephalai, Plutarch (*Flam.* 14.1) mentions Greek helmets and Macedonian *peltai* and *sarisai* being on display. Note that there is no reference to cuirasses in these panoplies.

Although the peltasts could and did fight in the phalanx on occasion, as at Pydna, their equipment was lighter than that of the phalangites: their bronze *peltai* shields were smaller, which enabled them to be used 'for special action, particularly in conjunction with light troops and mercenaries' (Walbank (1940) 292–3 with references).

Ivory-hilted iron dagger; the present preserved length is 21.4cm (8.4in), but the tip is obviously missing. A fragment of the rectangular scabbard chape has also been preserved. Purchased in Greece, this weapon had survived in such good condition that it probably came from a looted Hellenistic tomb. Daggers of this type were used by peltast units in a number of Hellenistic armies, and this one may originally have belonged to an officer of *peltastai*. (British Museum 1864.2–20.113; author's photo)

The *agēma*

Within the peltasts, the *agēma* or 'vanguard' constituted an elite. In battle the king would adopt a position between the Sacred Squadron and the *agēma* (Livy 42.58.9). In Livy's description (43.19.11) of the siege of Oaeneum during the winter campaigns of 169, he mentions that the city was taken by a siege-mound, used as a base of attack by 'the royal company (*cohors regia*) whom they call the Conquerors' (*Nicatores*). From the siege context it is clear that this must be an infantry unit, and the most rational assumption must be that it is the *agēma*. 'Conquerors' is clearly a nickname, but behind the Latin *cohors regia* may lie an alternative official title for the unit in Greek: perhaps *basilika syntagma*, as the word Livy uses regularly in Latin to translate the Greek *syntagma* is *cohors*.

The *regia cohors* is also mentioned in Livy's description (40.6.3) of the ritual purification of the army in 182, when the *regia cohors* marches at its head, a role that would befit its title of 'vanguard' regiment. Opinion on how to interpret the unit title is divided. Briscoe (2008: 426) concurs with previous editors that Livy means the royal pages when he uses this term. Elsewhere in Livy (44.43.5), however, the royal pages are called the *regii pueri*, so once again it seems that it is the *agēma* that is being referred to.

When the army was fielded at full strength the *agēma* numbered 2,000 and the 'other *peltastai*' 3,000. In describing the army review at Citium in 171 on the eve of the Third Macedonian War, Livy (42.51.4–5) mentions that the *agēma*, commanded by Leonnatos and Thrasyppos, consisted of 2,000 men chosen from all the *peltastai* 'for their strength and the enduring energy of their age' (*et viribus et robore aetatis*). This presumably means the men were veterans. Leonnatos and Thrasyppos probably held the rank of *chiliarchos*. The leader of the 'other *peltastai*', about 3,000 men, was Antiphilos of Edessa.

The formula 'the *agēma* and the other *peltastai*' can be restored in the conscription *diagramma* of Philip V (Juhel & Sekunda, 2009). Plutarch (*Aem.* 18.3) preserves an eyewitness account of their appearance at the battle of Pydna in 168 BC. The third unit to move into line is 'the *agēma*, picked men, the purest of the Macedonians on account of their virtue and age, gleaming with gilded weapons and newly-dyed crimson tunics'. This confirms that the *agēma* consisted of more senior men selected out of the ranks of the *peltastai*. The conscription *diagramma* of Philip V extends the maximum age for service in the *agēma* from 45 to 50, while that for service in the peltasts remained 35 years.

In lists of forces the *agēma* is frequently not listed separately, but as part of the *peltastai*. The strength at which the *peltastai* were deployed, and the strength of the *agēma* within it, varied over time, according to the level of mobilization for a particular campaign. At the start of the Social War in 219 they are listed with a full strength of 5,000 (Polyb. 4.29.1), but during the winter campaign later that year Philip took with him only 2,000 *peltastai* (Polyb. 4.67.6). Polybius (5.25.1) mentions a conspiracy that took place the next year in Corinth. Leontios, Megaleas and Ptolemaios spread a rumour among 'the *peltastai* and those belonging to what is called the *agēma* by the Macedonians'. At Kynoskephalai in 197 the *peltastai* numbered 2,000 (Livy 33.4.4–5), and Antigonos Doson had 3,000 *peltastai* at the battle of Sellasia in 222 (Polyb. 2.65).

The 2,000 light troops (*levium armorum*) Perseus took with him against Stuberra in the winter of 169 (Livy 43.18.4) are presumably skirmishers rather than the *peltastai*. In early 168 we find a garrison of 2,000 *peltastai* stationed at Thessaloniki under the command of Eumenes and Athenagoras – presumably *chiliarchoi* (Livy 44.32.6). The 2,000 'Macedonians' sent out before the battle on a special operation around Olympus together with 10,000 foreign mercenaries (including some Thracians armed with javelins) under the command of one Milo (Plut. *Aem.* 16.1), probably belonged to the *peltastai*. The *peltastai* fought in the second line behind the phalanx at Pydna (Livy 44.41.1–2), presumably at their full strength of 5,000.

The *chalkaspides*

Like the rest of the infantry, the *chalkaspides*, who made up the main body of the Macedonian phalanx, were organized into units of a thousand men. Polybius (2.65.2) mentions that the Macedonian infantry at Sellasia numbered 10,000 phalangites and 3,000 *peltastai*. The *chalkaspides* were drawn up on the slope of the Euas on the right, and on the opposite flank the mercenaries were drawn up in front, and then 'the rest of the Macedonians' – presumably the *peltastai* – drawn up in a double phalanx (2.66.8–9).

When the young Philip V first moved out of Macedonia at the beginning of 219 BC to take part in the Social War, he took with him 10,000 phalangites, 5,000 *peltastai* and 800 cavalry; all of them Macedonians (Polyb. 4.37.7). Later on in the winter Philip resumed the campaign with a much reduced force, taking about 400 elite cavalry, 300 Cretans, 2,000 *peltastai* and 3,000 *chalkaspides* (4.67.6).

At Kynoskephalai, Livy (33.4.4) states that the phalanx numbered 16,000, 'the enduring strength of all the men of the kingdom', and the *peltastai* 2,000. This strength was a maximum effort, only achieved by the lowering of the minimum age of service to 15, as mentioned in the 'conscription' decree probably enacted specifically for this campaign. Following the disaster at Kynoskephalai, where 8,000 Macedonians were killed and 5,000 captured (Polyb. 18.27.6; Livy 33.10.7), Philip was nevertheless able to raise an adequate force to counter the Dardanian invasion. He rapidly levied troops 'in the cities of Macedonia' up to a strength of 6,000 infantry and 500 cavalry (Livy 33.19.3). After Kynoskephalai, Philip's reign was an era of peace that did much to enlarge the Macedonian population (Livy 39.24.3–4). He passed on to his successor Perseus a much expanded army (42.11.6), and this was most noticeable in the strength of the phalanx.

Before the outbreak of the Third Macedonian war, King Eumenes of Pergamon, a long-standing enemy of Macedonia, had reported to the Roman Senate that King Perseus had laid aside a sufficient store of grain to feed 30,000 infantry and 5,000 cavalry (Livy 42.12.8). From this figure we must at least deduct the 5,000 men who served in the *agēma* and the other *peltastai*. In the review of the army in 171, Livy (42.51.3–11) says that there were 43,000 men under arms, of whom 'about half' were phalangites. Livy then lists the individual units of infantry other than the phalangites – 5,000 of the *agēma* and the other *peltastai*, 12,000 non-Macedonian mercenary or allied troops, and 1,000 Odrysian allied infantry – which gives a total of 39,000 infantry. This leaves a strength of 21,000 men for the phalanx. For the Pydna campaign itself in 168, Perseus had not much fewer than 40,000 infantry 'for the phalanx' (Plut,

*Aem.*13.3). The latter figure can be reconciled with the other sources only if it is a total figure for the infantry.

The *leukaspides*

It has been suggested that the Macedonian phalanx included a second regiment called the *leukaspides* or 'white shields'. Livy (44.41.1–2) tells us that in the later stages of the battle of Pydna, Aemilius Paulus achieved victory by placing his first legion in between the *peltastai* in the second line, and the phalanx of the *chalkaspides* in the first. To Aemilius' right, he continues, Lucius Albinus led the second legion against the *phalanx* of the *leukaspides* which formed the centre of the Macedonian line. The *leukaspides* are not referred to in the account of the battle left by Plutarch, although in their place he mentions the Thracians, who are dressed in black tunics and are equipped with *rhomphaias*, white *thureoi* and greaves (Plut. *Aem. Paul.* 18.2). Livy is probably referring to these Thracians carrying white *thureoi* when he refers to the phalanx of the *leukaspides*.

Diodorus (31.8.10) states that in the triumph Aemilius Paulus celebrated after the battle there were 1,200 wagons filled with white shields (further qualified as *tracheias*, 'rough') and a further 1,200 wagons filled with bronze shields. The parallel account in Plutarch (*Aem. Paul.* 32) mentions Thracian shields being carried in wagons at the triumph, so the white shields mentioned by Diodorus might have been the white *thureoi* carried by the Thracians.

Plutarch (*Cleom.* 23.1) states that before the battle of Sellasia, Kleomenes III of Sparta created a second Lakedaimonian phalanx by arming 2,000 freed helots 'in the Macedonian fashion as a counter to the *leukaspides*'. We should neither assume from this passage that the *leukaspides* fighting on the Macedonian side were armed 'in Macedonian fashion', nor that they were necessarily ethnic Macedonians. At this battle the *chalkaspides* were drawn up on the right in alternate *speirai* along with the Illyrians (2.66.5), who numbered 1,600 (2.65.4). The Illyrians were probably armed with *thureoi*, which were generally faced with white felt at this period. This may be the *leukaspides* Kleomenes had in mind when arming the 2,000 emancipated helots.

Probably, therefore, all the references to a phalanx of *leukaspides* serving in the Macedonian army are to formations of *thureophoroi* who were not ethnically Macedonian. A regiment of *leukaspides* is mentioned for the first time in the Tarentine army commanded by Pyrrhos of Epirus at the battle of Asculum in 279 BC (Dion. Hal. 20.1.2–4). Though the date is very early, this might also refer to a formation of *thureophoroi*.

ARTILLERY

Ever since the reign of Philip II the Macedonians had been experts in using catapults (dart-throwers) and *ballistai* (stone-throwers), in the field as well as in siege operations. On campaign in Epirus in 198, Philip V first contemplated using his artillery against the Romans across a river that separated the two forces. He later withdrew to a line of cliffs, and ranged his catapults and *ballistai* upon them 'as if on a wall' (Livy 32.10.9). In 171, the army was accompanied by an enormous number of wagons to carry the catapults and the huge supply of missiles that were to be shot from them (Livy 42.53.4). Following the surrender of three Thessalian cities out of fear, King Perseus took the fourth one by storm. In the final campaign against the Romans, fought in the vicinity of Pydna in 168, the Macedonians fortified the banks of the River Elpeius so strongly that the Roman consul opposing them regarded the riverbank as impregnable 'by nature and by fortification', and, besides the fact that artillery had been placed everywhere, 'he had heard that the enemy employed missile weapons better and with more deadly aim' (Livy 44.35.10).

A new weapon, the *kestrosphendone* or 'dart-sling', described by Livy (42.65.9–10) and Polybius (27.11), came into use for the first time in 171. The dart, which was shot from a sling, had an iron head 9in long set in an inch-thick wooden shaft of equal length, which was fitted on the outside with three short fir-wood flights.

SELECT BIBLIOGRAPHY

Andronicos, Manolis, 'Sarissa', in *Bulletin de Correspondance Héllénique* 94 (1970) 91–107

Arvanitopoulos, A.S., *Graptai Stēlai Demetriados-Pagasōn* (Athens, 1928)

Blinkenberg, Chr. & K.F. Kinch, *Lindos Fouilles de l'Acropole 1902–1914 II Inscriptions, Tome 1* (Berlin, Copenhagen, 1941)

Briscoe, John, 'The *cognomen Philippus*', in *Gerión* 2 (1984) 151–3

Briscoe, John, *A Commentary on Livy Books 38–40* (Oxford, 2008)

Connolly, Peter, 'Experiments with the *sarissa*, the Macedonian pike and cavalry lance – a functional view', in *Journal of Roman Military Equipment Studies* 11 (2000) 103–112

Charbonneaux, J., R. Martin & F. Villard, *Hellenistic Art 330–50 BC* (London, 1973)

Feyel, M., 'Un nouveau fragment du règlement militaire trouvé à Amphipolis', in *Revue archéologique* (1935, 2) 29–68

Gauthier, Ph. & M.B. Hatzopoulos, *La Loi gymnasiarchique de Béroia* (=ΜΕΛΕΤΗΜΑΤΑ 16, Athens, 1993)

Goukowsky, Paul, 'Makedonika', in *Revue des Études Grecques* 100 (1987) 239–55

Hammond, N.G.L., 'A Cavalry Unit in the Army of Antigonus Monophthalmus: *Asthippoi*', in *Classical Quarterly* 28 (1978) 128–34

Hammond, N.G.L., 'A Macedonian Shield and Macedonian Measures', in *Annual of the British School at Athens* 91 (1996) 365–7

Hatzopoulos, M.B., *Une donation du roi Lysimaque* (= ΜΕΛΕΤΗΜΑΤΑ 5, Athens, 1988)

Hatzopoulos, M.B., *Macedonian Institutions under the Kings*, I–II (= ΜΕΛΕΤΗΜΑΤΑ 22, Athens, 1996)

Hatzopoulos, M.N., *L'organisation de l'armée macédonienne sous les Antigonides. Problèmes anciens et documents nouveaux* (= ΜΕΛΕΤΗΜΑΤΑ 30, Athens, 2001)

Juhel, Pierre, '"On orderliness with respect to the prizes of war": the Amphipolis regulation and the management of booty in the army of the last Antigonids', in *Annual of the British School at Athens* 97 (2002) 401–12, pl. 37–8

Juhel, Pierre, 'Fragments de "boucliers macédoniens" au nom de Roi Démétrios trouvés à Staro Bonce (République de Macédoine)', in *Zeitschrift für Papyrologie und Epigrafik* 162 (2007) 165–80

Juhel, Pierre, 'The Regulation Helmet of the Phalanx and the Introduction of the Concept of Uniform in the Macedonian Army at the End of the Reign of Alexander the Great', in *Klio* 91, 2 (2009) 342–55

Juhel, P. & N.V. Sekunda, 'The *agema* and "the other peltasts" in the late Antigonid Army, and in the Drama/Cassandreia Conscription *diagramma*', in *Zeitschrift für Papyrologie und Epigrafik* 170 (2009) 104–108

Juhel, Pierre, 'La Stèle funéraire d'Amyntas fils d'Alexandre, cavalier des confins macédoniens', in *Acta Archaeologica* 81 (2010) 112–17

Juhel, P. & Dule Temelkoski, 'Découverte de nouveaux « boucliers macédoniens » en Pélagonie (République de Macédoine). Aspects archéologiques et réflexions historiques', in Jean-Christophe Couvenhes, Sandrine Crouzet et Sandra Péré-Nogues (ed.), *Pratiques*

et identités culturelles des armées hellénistiques du monde méditerranéen: Actes du Troisième Congrès international Hellenistic Warfare, Tours, 23 et 24 mars 2007 (Bordeaux, 2011) 177–91.

Kähler, Heinz, *Der Fries vom Reiterdenkmal des Aemilius Paullus in Delphi* (Berlin, 1965)

Liampi, Katerina, *Der makedonische Schild* (Bonn, 1998)

Mathisen, R.W., 'The Shield/Helmet Bronze Coinage of Macedonia: a Preliminary Analysis', in *Journal of the Society of Ancient Numismatics* 10 (1979) 2–6

Miller, Stella G., *The Tomb of Lyson and Kallikles: a Painted Macedonian Tomb* (Mainz, 1993)

Noguera Borel, A., 'L'évolution de la phalange macédonienne: le cas de la sarisse', in *Ancient Macedonia, Sixth International Symposium, Volume 2* (Thessaloniki, 1999) 839–50

Pandermalis, D., 'Basile[ōs Dēmētr]iou', in *Myrtos. Mnēme Ioulias Vokotopoulou* (Thessaloniki, 2000) xviii–xxii

Petsas, Ph., *O Taphos tōn Lefkadiōn* (Athens, 1966)

Proeva, Nade, 'Des Plaques de Ceintures provenant des Contrées illyriennes et de Dassarétie', in Jean-Luc Lamboley & Maria Paola Castiglioni (ed.), *L'Illyrie Méridionele et l'Épire dans l'Antiquité – V, Actes du Ve colloque international de Grenoble (8–11 octobre 2008)* Vol. II (Paris, 2011) 577–89

Ragghianti, Carlo Ludovico, *Pittori di Pompei* (Milan, 1963)

Reinach, A.J., 'La frise du monument de Paul-Émile à Delphes', in *Bulletin de Correspondance Hellénique* 34 (1910) 444–6

Robinson, D.M., Excavations at Olynthus, Part X Metal and Minor Miscellaneous Finds (Baltimore, 1941)

Roisman, Joseph & Ian Worthington, *A Companion to Ancient Macedonia* (Oxford, 2010).

Roussel, P., 'Un règlement militaire de l'époque macédonienne', in *Revue Archéologique* (1934, 1) 39–47

Sabin, Philip, Hans Van Wees & Michael Whitby, *The Cambridge History of Greek and Roman Warfare. Volume I: Greece, the Hellenistic World and the Rise of Rome* (Cambridge, 2007)

Sekunda, Nicholas & Angus McBride, *The Army of Alexander the Great* (Osprey MAA 148, London, 1984)

Sekunda, Nicholas, 'The Sarissa', in *Acta Universitatis Lodziensis, Folia Archaeologica* 23 (2001) 13–41

Sekunda, Nicholas, 'A Macedonian Companion in a Pompeian Fresco', in *Archeologia* (Warsaw) 54 (2003) 29–33 pl. x–xi

Tziafalias, Athanasios & Bruno Helly, 'Inscriptions de la Tripolis de Perrhébie. Lettres Royales de Démétrios II et Antigone Dôsôn', in *Studia Hellenistica* 24 (2010) 71–125

Tsimbidou-Avloniti, Maria, *Makedonikoi Taphoi ston Phoinika kai ston Agio Athanasio Thessalonikis* (Athens, 2005)

Walbank, F.W., *Philip V of Macedon* (Cambridge, 1940), 'Appendix II: Notes on the Army under Philip V', pp. 289–94.

Welles, C. Bradford, 'New texts from the chancery of Philip V of Macedonia and the problem of the "diagramma"', in *American Journal of Archaeology* 42 (1938) 245–60

PLATE COMMENTARIES

A: CAVALRY INSPECTION, c.325–300 BC

Figures A1 and A3 are based two similar Pompeian frescos from the 'House of Jason' and the 'The House of the Golden Cupids', reproducing a painting of the 4th century BC (Sekunda, 2003).

A1 wears the Boeotian helmet that continued to be popular in the earliest years of the Hellenistic period. A saffron-yellow Macedonian cloak with a purple border was a distinguishing feature of the 'Companions' cavalry under Alexander, and this individual presumably belonged to the elite cavalry regiment of the Antipatrid army, successors to the Companions. He wears a sky-blue long-sleeved tunic, with a 'double overfall' (belted twice at the waist, and folding over both belts). Alexander's Companions are shown wearing a single-belted overfall, and the double overfall seems to be a slightly later Macedonian court fashion – perhaps dating the original painting to the last couple of decades of the 4th century? The long-sleeved tunic (*chiton cheiridotos*), Persian in origin, went out of fashion quite soon after the death of Alexander, who had tried to establish a system of joint Macedonian–Persian rule; consequently the garment lost its earlier ideological significance. The boots, which are a light purplish-grey in colour, reach to mid-calf and are reminiscent of Thracian footwear (*embades*); they have a roll of leather or felt at the top, attached to which are yellow hanging lappets that taper towards the bottom. These boots are made of whole pieces of leather instead of the usual strap-work, and are laced internally. It is not known whether the horse-furniture was issued or purchased privately, but it has been restored with colours to match the tunic and cloak.

A2 is based on a figure from the 'Bella' Tomb, and probably represents a senior officer of an elite cavalry unit. He wears a medium-blue sleeveless tunic under a composite cuirass of purple and white plates. The purple chest-plate bears the golden head of a bearded male figure – either Pan, or a satyr. The shoulder-guards are purple with a narrow gold border but are otherwise plain (any decoration in the central area can no longer be made out in the source). Wrapped around his waist is a cloak (*ephaptis*) of a type normally worn by infantrymen. The boots are untypical, and seem to consist of a 'shoe' part and a 'gaiter' part, fastened with long laces. The spear has a large bronze butt similar in shape to the one now preserved in the Great North Museum, Newcastle upon Tyne.

A3 is based on the same sources as A1, which represents the mythological figure of Jason. His crimson cloak has a sky-blue border, and is probably a semicircular garment of the Macedonian type. The combination of crimson and blue are colours frequently associated with the infantry, suggesting that Jason is depicted dressed as a senior infantry officer, in 'off-duty' dress and holding a walking-stick in his right hand.

B: GUARD CAVALRY REGIMENT, c.325–300 BC

Nearly all the figures in our Plates B–E are based on the Agios Athanasios Tomb, dating to the last quarter of the 4th century BC (Tsimbidou-Avloniti (2005) 108). This tomb, discovered in 1994, lies close to Thessaloniki at the site of the ancient Herakleia on Axios. None of the figures depicted in the tomb wear the long-sleeved tunic, which indicates that by the end of the 4th century it had been abandoned as a feature of Macedonian military and court dress in favour of the traditional sleeveless tunic. The tomb appears to be of slightly later date than the 'Bella' Tomb (see A2).

These three figures all wear saffron-yellow Macedonian cloaks with purple borders (a distinguishing mark of the elite Macedonian cavalry regiment), the latter edged with a narrow gold line. All three wear white *kausiai* headgear. **B1** and **B3** wear composite cuirasses, of which the outermost layer is of purple-dyed leather. They are decorated with what appear to be thunderbolt motifs on the shoulder-guards, and two narrow gold lines at the ends of the two sets of groin-flaps. Pairs of similar gold lines also decorate the 'belt' and breastplate of the cuirass, although the details are difficult to make out. All three figures wear boots consisting of felt 'socks' (with separate big toes) coloured off-white, held in place with a 'frame' of medium-brown straps which finish in two knotted laces at the top.

All three men wear tunics of different colours – white with red bands woven into the cloth in the case of **B1,** and plain medium-blue and white respectively in the case of **B2** and **B3.** The difference may have been a personal choice, or perhaps depended on the sub-unit of the regiment to which the individual belonged. Another figure in the main fresco from the Agios Athanasios tomb appears in a non-military context wearing a cloak of the same colour combination and dressed in a red tunic.

All three men carry small spears, with iron leaf-shaped blades but apparently without metal butts. Only **B3** is shown with a sword, though all but the hilt is hidden by his cloak. The hilt is ivory or (more probably) bone. It has a cylindrical pommel, decorated near the top with a narrow ring of yellow metal, and a barrel-shaped hand-grip also of white bone secured by two yellow-metal decorative inlays, presumably covering rivets. The sword hangs on a narrow baldric of yellow or light brown leather.

C: ROYAL PAGE AND HEAVY CAVALRYMEN, c.325–300 BC

C1 represents a Royal Page, and is based on the somewhat later grave stele of Stratonikos from Demetrias (see page 39), and on two Pompeian frescoes depicting the 'Embarkation of Helen', all three of which show juvenile figures in white cloaks and brown tunics. The boots are open-toed and of white leather, held in place at the top by double brown leather 'gapters'. When outdoors the Royal Pages would have worn a *kausia*, presumably in white to match their cloaks.

The two other figures both wear medium-brown Macedonian cloaks with purple borders (without any narrow line at the edge). Both wear strap-work boots of the usual cavalry variety. Otherwise **C3** is shown in only a white tunic, without *kausia*, cuirass or spear, but presumably he would normally have worn all these items. **C2** has a white *kausia*, a medium-blue tunic, and a composite cuirass of a type identical to those worn by B1 and B3; this was presumably issued to all the heavy cavalry regiments of the Macedonian national army at that time. He carries a cavalry spear of the same type as the heavy cavalrymen in Plate B. Again, the variety of tunic colour could be explained by individual preference or difference in sub-unit. Other figures shown in a non-military context in the main fresco from the Agios Athanasios Tomb wear medium brown Macedonian cloaks with purple borders, and red and white tunics.

Several other figures in the fresco wear blue Macedonian cloaks with a purple border; their tunics are of white material with bands of yellow woven in, and purple with narrow white vertical stripes down both sides. These might perhaps represent members of a third Macedonian national cavalry regiment appearing unarmed and in 'undress' as revellers, although Macedonian cloaks might equally be worn by civilians.

It is not known whether the three **shields** hanging on the wall behind belonged to the Macedonian army or were captured from their enemies. The one on the left is based on a fresco from the 'Bella' Tomb, showing a hoplite shield with its distinctive bronze offset rim, and a white-painted field with a small red medallion decorated with a golden-brown feathered harpy. Those at centre and right both come from the Agios Athanasios Tomb, painted on the wall above the two figures shown in Plate D. Both of them might be hoplite shields, but this is doubtful. Although the same size as hoplite shields, both appear to be flat, made of wood or leather with metal rims. It would be tempting to think both were cavalry shields, but this would place the introduction of the cavalry shield before the currently accepted date of the 270s BC.

The shield in the centre is painted with a Medusa's head of unknown significance, on a purple field, all within a wide bronze rim which is extremely curved in section. The shield on the right is decorated with a highly stylized winged thunderbolt, which (along with that of figure E2) seems to be the first appearance of the winged thunderbolt as a shield-device in ancient iconography, as has been pointed out to me by Valery Nikonorov. At first glance it is shown back to front in the Tomb fresco, with the spear of the cavalryman passing through an iron *porpax* (which should make it a hoplite shield shown from the back). This is probably best explained by faulty work on the part of the artist, who painted the blue colour last. He has elsewhere mistakenly shown the cavalry spear passing underneath the shield's narrow iron rim. (Painters working in fresco had to work quickly before the plaster dried.) Furthermore, the *porpakes* of hoplite shields were generally bronze, and the iron grip of a thunderbolt is being shown on the shield. It would, in any case, make little sense to show shields hung back-to-front on a wall.

D: LIGHT CAVALRY, c.325–300 BC

This plate reconstructs the two figures flanking the entrance to the Agios Athanasios Tomb. Their boots indicate that they are cavalrymen, otherwise they would be shown barefoot. Both wear the rectangular Thessalian cloak, which signifies that they are ethnic Thessalians. The ancients attached great importance to the 'hang' of their garments, and both horsemen's cloaks have small lead weights sewn to each of their four corners.

D1 wears a cloak of light pinkish brick-red colour, with a broad white border edged with a narrow line in the same colour as the body of the cloak. **D2's** cloak is of similar design but in black and white. Both men wear dark grey tunics, with white

Bronze helmet of the 'Phrygian' type, from archaeological excavations at Vitsa, Macedonia. Compare this piece with Plate E2; note the tube for a side plume, and the fittings at the front of the crest. Judging by the Agios Athanassios Tomb, various units of Macedonian infantry based in Europe continued to use the 'Phrygian' helmet for at least a decade or two after Alexander's death. As throughout history, a serviceable piece of armour would seldom be discarded without good reason. (Ioannina Museum)

vertical stripes of different widths. These stripes are also a sign that the two men are in paid service, that is mercenaries; similar stripes normally appear on the tunics of men in paid service – such as *paidagōgoi*, for example, paid freed men who accompanied boys to and from school. The minor differences in cloak colours and other dress details indicate that the two men belong to two separate units, both recruited in Thessaly. They wear white *kausiai*, in this case simply indicating that they are in Macedonian service. Their lances are *xysta*, unusually without butt-spikes; it is possible that the two horsemen belong to two units of Thessalian *xystophoroi* (lancers), who would fight without shields or body-armour.

E: INFANTRYMEN OF THE GUARD, c.325–300 BC

All three figures shown in this plate probably belong to the Macedonian regiment of foot-guards, given the prevalence of purple, in which case **E2** would belong to the elite *chiliarchia* of the three that comprised that regiment.

Again, the significance of the differently coloured tunics is unknown. In the case of **E2** the tunic is red. The tunics worn by the other two are of a rare type that I have not been able to identify, in which bands of colour (yellow in the case of **E1**, and red in **E3**) are woven into the white background cloth.

The shield of **E1** has a white rim and an outer field painted red with three double crescents with an elongated dot in the centre, separated by thunderbolts, all painted in gold. The purple centre, surrounded by a white ring, is decorated with a stylized starburst painted in gold. Opposite the thunderbolts on the outer field the rays are narrower and shorter, and opposite the crescents they are longer and widen towards the centre of the starburst, which has a dot.

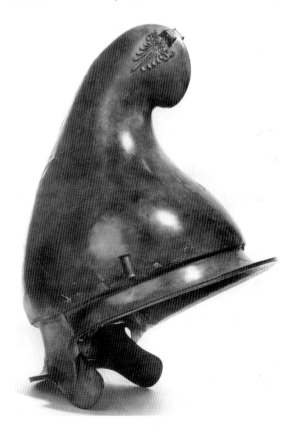

E2's 'Phrygian' shaped helmet is of polished bronze; it is decorated with a central crest, probably of horsehair dyed purple, and two white wing-feathers taken from a large bird, probably a goose. The purple centre of his shield, surrounded by a white ring, is decorated with a golden thunderbolt, indicating his status as belonging to an elite sub-unit. The medium-blue outer field is decorated with six sets of double crescents with pellets in the centre, again alternating with thunderbolts.

E3 also wears a 'Phrygian' helmet, but painted purple. It is again decorated with two side-feathers, but lacks a central crest. His shield has a red rim and a white outer field decorated with eight sets of double crescents with pellets in the middle. The centre of the shield is very faint, which led to the present author's mistaken earlier identification with the white shields of the *leukaspides* (Sabin, Van Wees & Whitby (2007) 338). It is in fact blue, with a (probably) 12-rayed starburst painted in yellow. Again, the radii of the starburst are shown as alternating between narrower, shorter rays and longer ones widening towards the centre. The boots are unusual for an infantryman, but are paralleled by Alexandrine *hypaspistai* (see Sekunda & McBride, MAA 148, *The Army of Alexander the Great* (1984) Plate E1 – whose shield I now realize should be decorated with a starburst).

All three figures carry infantry *sarisai*, though only E3 has a sword – presumably the others have laid theirs aside for convenience.

F: THE MACEDONIAN ARMY, *c.*280 BC

F1 is based on the Lefkadia Tomb published by Petsas in 1966. Once again, the saffron-yellow cloak with purple border identifies the deceased as a soldier of the elite cavalry regiment of the Macedonian national army. Figures F2 and F3 are based on a Pompeian fresco from 'The House of the Menander', which copies a painting originally produced for the Macedonian court in around 280 BC. We have reconstructed them as if attending a sacrifice outside the doors of a palace.

F2 is based on the figure of Ajax in the fresco, clearly carrying the equipment of a Macedonian peltast. He is depicted barefoot, and clad in a pinkish-red tunic of a crimson hue with a light blue border. Scipio Nasica, an eyewitness of the battle of Pydna in 168 BC, states that the *agēma* wore newly-made crimson tunics at the battle (Plut., *Aem. Paul.* 18.3). The Greeks tended to describe colours by their tint rather than their hue. Thus the word *phoenix* (usually translated incorrectly as 'scarlet'), can be used for crimson, represented by a range

Fresco from the 'House of the Menander' in Pompeii, showing the fall of Troy, and believed to be copied from one of the original 3rd-century paintings by Theoros of Samos. On the left, King Menelaus (see Plate F3) drags his wife Helen back to the Greek camp by her hair, while on the right Ajax the lesser (see Plate F2) is pulling his daughter Cassandra from the altar of Athena; King Priam stands helplessly in the centre. (Photo Roger Ling)

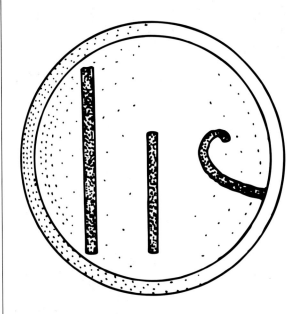

of colours from purple to pink, so long as it has a blue-ish tint to it. Our pinkish tunic does not conflict with Plutarch – quite the opposite. Plutarch describes these tunics as 'newly-made', presumably because they had only recently been issued to the regiment. The light blue tunic border is probably a distinction common to infantry units, just as Alexander's infantry were distinguished by their blue helmets. Peltasts normally wore helmets, but in the fresco Ajax wears a white felt cap shaped like a short sugar-loaf; such caps would have been worn as padding under the helmet. Several other representations show peltasts wearing similar caps, which suggests that it was frequent practice to discard the uncomfortable helmet.

Ajax carries over his left shoulder a pike that has been shortened by the Pompeian artist to fit the composition. The shield has a narrow bronze rim on its inside. Its outer surface would also have been sheet bronze, decorated with the geometric patterns of the 'Macedonian' shield. Happily, the inside of the *peltē* is seen here, faced in white leather, and it shows how the shield was held. Three leather strap-handles are attached to the back of the shield. The first is held together with the pike-shaft, by the index finger of the left hand. The second handle, passing over the left forearm just above the wrist, runs vertically across the middle of the shield, in the form of a leather strap about an inch across and 8in long; it is attached asymmetrically, from just above the shield's centre to just above the bottom. A third handle runs vertically to the left of the second, crossing the forearm just below the elbow; partially obscured by Ajax's upper arm, it seems to be somewhat longer that the middle handle. The peltasts at Pydna would have marched to battle with their *peltai* slung over their shoulders by means of this third strap. His dagger has a white handle, presumably of bone; no baldric is shown, so the dagger must have been worn on a waist-belt. The hilt

has a pommel and a barrel-shaped grip apparently made from a single piece; a white rectangle below these in the painting is probably the mouth of the sheath, also white.

F3 depicts the Macedonian king who is represented in the fresco as King Menelaus. The purple cloak and tunic (edged in blue) clearly indicate a royal personage. His purple-crested helmet is fitted with a pair of bull's horns, as first adopted by Demetrios Poliorketes as the attributes of Poseidon, who had granted him victory in the sea-battle off Salamis. However, the monarch in this painting is a rather unattractive man, while Demetrios was reputedly very handsome. It must rather show his quite ugly son Antigonos Gonatas, who was born around 320 BC. Antigonos is known from other representations to have worn bull's horns on his helmet prior to his adoption of the goat's horns of Pan in 277 BC. He carries a Macedonian shield of a type shown on coins from the early part of his reign; note the blazon of an 'ANT' monogram.

G: LYSON AND KALLIKLES, c.222 BC

The tomb of Lyson and Kallikles was discovered in 1942 by C.I. Makaronas at Lefkadia, and was published by Dr Stella G. Miller in 1993. One Euippos, son of Aristophanes, constructed the tomb to preserve the remains of his brothers Lyson and Kallikles, whose names are written on the lintel over the burial chamber entrance. The cremated remains of all three brothers were interred in three niches in the north wall opposite the entrance – Euippos on the left, Lyson in the centre, and Kallikles on the right. The tomb paintings include very detailed depictions of two sets of war-gear, which we reconstruct here on the two figures.

G1 is an officer of the Macedonian guard cavalry regiment. He is obviously the more important and perhaps the elder of the two brothers, and may be Lyson – whose remains occupied the central niche in the north wall, and who is mentioned first in the dedicatory inscription. We have given him cavalry boots, a red tunic, and a saffron-yellow cloak with purple border and corner weights, appropriate for his regiment. The fact that the cavalry helmet is yellow (with a red stripe) confirms the regimental identification. The red plume also seems to be part of the regimental uniform. A further facing colour, black, is shown as a second band and trimming on the helmet, and as piping on the *pteruges* of the cuirass. The white lateral helmet plumes are probably badges of rank. The shield is decorated with a star and a wreath of laurel or myrtle. The eight-pointed star constantly recurs as a symbol in Macedonian contexts, though its significance remains unclear. The wreath is a traditional symbol of victory, which was later awarded as a distinction to Roman cavalry units.

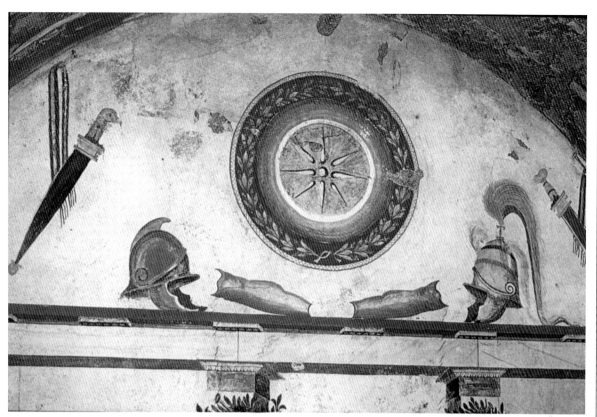

G2 is a member of the *chalkaspides*, possibly Kallikles. The absence of any plumes makes his rank uncertain, but officer status is probably indicated by the gilt edging to his helmet. The navy-blue and red colour combination on the helmet and the piping of the *pteruges* (groin-flaps) would be suitable 'infantry colours'. A red tunic has been restored, as have the sandals and greave-garters. The red helmet has a comb crest, and is of a type worn by a Macedonian infantryman carrying a bronze embossed Macedonian shield on the Aemilius Paulus Monument. This allows us to associate the red helmet, and the cuirass that goes with it, with the bronze shield, which in turn allows us to identify the soldier as belonging to the *chalkaspides*. The infantry greaves must also belong to this

figure. They are of a type found in the Hellenistic period, reaching to above the knee like contemporary Roman greaves; they had to be left open behind the knee to let the leg articulate, and so were normally held in place by garters above the ankle and below the knee.

It is clear that the same two swords are shown on each lunette, but reversed. The 'ear-shaped' pommel is coloured differently on each side – presumably deliberately, rather than by artistic error. The baldric of this sword is not duplicated accurately, and it seems that the artist has negligently transferred the black and blue of the baldric of the eagle-hilted sword to that with the 'eared' pommel when depicting the rear of the latter. Swords with ear-shaped pommels are extremely

Herm of Philip V wearing a helmet adorned with ram's horns spiralling out from each brow, and a low central horsehair crest that curves forward in rounded tufts. The helmet has a sharply defined ridge recalling the edge of a *kausia*, and below this it extends downwards onto the forehead. It is fitted with cheek-pieces, presumably hinged, and a highly complicated nape-protector adorned with ram's heads.
The carving also shows two lappets, derived from the hood traditional to Perseus, that hang down in front of the shoulders of the cuirass. See Plate H1. (Courtesy of the Syndics of the Fitzwilliam Museum, Cambridge)

common during the Hellenistic period, and it seems reasonable that they were used by regiments of the line. Swords with animal-head hilts, though not rare, are far less common. The ornate nature of the eagle-head hilt, apparently in cast bronze, suggests that it belonged to the cavalryman, so the sword with the ear-shaped hilt belongs to the infantryman.

The tomb was used for three generations only, and so for roughly 90 years or so. The letter-forms of the last inscription point to a date in the mid-2nd century, so the tomb was probably abandoned during the Andriskos uprising or following the deportations after Pydna. The fact that the bronze shield in the tomb paintings has – remarkably – no central blazon allows us to speculate that the tomb was built during the reign of Antigonos Doson (229–221 BC), who ruled as regent for the infant Philip V following the death of Demetrios II. Shields without blazons may have been issued to the army to signify the new monarch's constitutional status. Therefore, Lyson and Kallikles may both have died at the battle of Sellasia in 222.

H: KING PHILIP V, AND AMYNTAS, SON OF ALEXANDROS, 197 BC

H1 is based on two images of Philip V. The first is his equestrian portrait on a Roman *denarius* struck by Quintus Marcius Philippus in 129 BC. A Roman aristocrat of that name visited Philip V on an embassy in 183, and, it seems, received tokens of 'guest-friendship' in the form of portraits or sculptures, which in turn later appear on Roman *denarii* struck by his identically named descendant, presumably his grandson.

King Philip is clothed almost entirely in purple, as befits his royal status. Philip V's likeness is also preserved in a series of busts, derived from an original prototype which was also possibly once displayed in the 'Porticoes of Philippus'; these busts add to our knowledge of the accoutrements worn by Philip on the head and upper torso. In 214 BC, while staying in Argos at the house of Aratos, general of the Achaian League, the 23-year-old King Philip seduced, abducted, and then married Polykrateia, the wife of his host's son (also named Aratos). The Macedonian royal house claimed descent from the Argive hero Perseus; henceforward Philip identified closely with his divine ancestor, after whom he named his first son. After his experiences in Argos, Philip wore a helmet recalling the shape of a *kausia*, adorned with the lappets of the Persian hood normally seen in depictions of Perseus, and with the horns of a ram. The significance of this last element has yet to be explained, but the fact that Philip's helmet was horned is confirmed by a passage in Livy (27.33.2). This states that in 208 BC, during a raid on Sikyon, he was dashed against a tree by his charging horse, and broke off one of the two horns of his helmet.

H2 is based on the funerary stele of Amyntas, son of Alexandros, who probably died at the time of the Second Macedonian War against Rome (Juhel (2010) 117). The battle was fought in fog – thus Polybius 18.20.7: 'all the mist descended from the clouds on the earth, so that owing to the

Right side and front of a helmet (original findspot unknown), inscribed with the name 'Menophilou'. The helmet worn by Amyntas on his badly damaged grave stele found near Trebenište, north of Lake Ochrid, seems to be of similar shape – see Plate H2. (That region was annexed to the Macedonian kingdom in 217 BC but soon lost in 196 after the defeat of Kynoskephalai, which suggests a fairly narrow window for the date of Amyntas's death.) The helmet has two indentations in the brim on either side, which was the distinguishing feature of the earlier Boeotian form – the cavalry helmet *par excellence* – see Plate A1. In vestigial form these indentations survive on the cavalry helmet painted in the Tomb of Lyson and Kallikles – see Plate G1. (Ashmolean Museum, Oxford, 1971.904)

darkness that prevailed one could not see even people who were close at hand'.

Although the stele is badly damaged, it seems that Amyntas wears a conical helmet surmounted by what appears to be a single central plume and two hanging down at the sides that presumably indicate his officer status (compare with G1). The cuirass seems to be made of scales and fitted with a double row of *pteruges* hanging from the waist; Philip V also wears a scale cuirass, indicating a switch in design from the bronze plate type depicted in the tomb of Lyson and Kallikles. It is not clear whether Amyntas's cuirass is fitted with shoulder-guards, or if he wears a sword-belt. He carries a spear in his right hand, and has what appears to be a cloak wrapped around his left hand. A diminutive figure at Amyntas' left, his son or a slave, holds his shield, which is very large, round, and has a rim decorated with a wreath of olive leaves with the leaves running downwards – the opposite direction from that of G1. Less than half of the shield's surface is shown on the stele, but the blazon is clearly a thunderbolt with eight (or more) prongs. The rays of the thunderbolt curve out from the centre towards the rim, at first thickening but then narrowing into spear-like points; the thunderbolt may have had central wings, as shown in Plate C. The centre of the shield is not shown, but would probably have had a large central 'barley-corn' *umbo* and a *spina*. Since the shield of Amyntas has a wreath and thunderbolt, while that of Lyson (G1) has a wreath and star, it is likely that they belonged to different regiments, wearing differently coloured clothing.

INDEX

References to illustrations are shown in **bold**. Plates are shown with page and caption locators in brackets.

Achaian League 4, 5
Aemilius Paulus 36, 37; Monument **14**, **19**, 19, **23**, 46
Agios Athanasios Tomb 41, 42
Aitolia 5
Akrocorinth 4
Alexander (governor of Corinth) 4
Alexander III 'the Great', King 3, 7, 9, 20
Alexander IV, King 3, 4, 8
Alexandrine army 7
Alexandros, son of Admetos **37**
Amphipolis inscription 6, 8
Amyntas (*sōmatophylax*) 7
Amyntas, son of Andromenes 9
Amyntas, son of Alexandros **H2**(32, 47), **47**
Andronikos (*sōmatophylax*) 7
Antigonid army 6, 7
Antigonid dynasty 4–6, 7
Antigonos I Monophthalmos, King 3, 4
Antigonos II Gonatas, King 4, **17**, **18**, 19, 44
Antigonos III Doson, King 4, 5, 34, 47
Antimachos III, King of Bactria **10**
Antipatrid dynasty 3–4
Antipatros, King 3, 4, 11
Antiphanes 9, 10
Argead dynasty 3, 4
army staff 7–8
artillery 37
Asclepiodotus 18
Attalos 5

belt-plaque, bronze **5**
'bodyguards' (*sōmatophylakes*) 7
boots 6, 9, **10**, **13**, **A1**, **A2**(25, 41), **B**(26, 41), **C1**(27, 41–42)

cavalry 8–13; c.280 BC **F**(30, 43–44); clothing and equipment 8–9 *see also individual entries*; guard cavalry officer **G1**(31, 44, 46–47); guard cavalry regiment **B**(26, 41); heavy **C2**, **C3**(27, 41–42); horses 9, 10; *ilai* (units) 12; inspection **A**(25, 41); light **D**(28, 42); officers **12**, **G1**(31, 44, 46–47); organization 12–13; recruitment 9–10; regimental titles 10–11; *sacra ala* ('sacred squadron') 11, 12, 13; strength 12–13
cavalrymen **13**, **14**; heavy **C2**, **C3**(27, 41–42)
Chios, sea battle of (201) 5
'Chremonidean' war (267–255) 4
'Companions' (*hetairoi*) 7, 9, 10, 11, **A1**(25, 41)
cloaks: 'Macedonian' 8, **11**, **A1**(25, 41), **B**(26, 41), **C2**, **C3**(27, 41–42), **F**(30, 43–44); Thessalian **D**(28, 42)
coins 10, **17**, **18**, 18–19, **22**; *denarius* 6, **13**, **17**; 'shield/helmet' 4, **18**, **19**; tetradrachm **7**, **8**
cuirasses 3, 6, **11**, **12**, **A2**(25, 41), **B**(26, 41), **C2**(27, 41–42), **G**(31, 44, 46–47)

Demetrias 4
Demetrios I Poliorketes, King 3, **4**, 4, **10**, 44
Demetrios II, King 4, 5
diadem **10**

Eumenes, King of Pergamon 35

'friends' (*philoi*) 7

Galatian barbarians 4, 7
generals (*Diadochoi*) 3
Gonnoi decree 37
grammateus (secretary) 10, 24

hegēmon (file-leader) **3**, **21**, 21
Helen of Troy **9**, **43**
helmets **17**; Amyntas' **G2**(31, 44, 46–47), **47**; 'Attic' type **11**; Boeotian **A1**(25, 41); cavalry **13**, **G1**(31, 44, 46–47), **44**; horned **G1**(31, 44, 46–47), **46**; infantry 20, **23**, **G2**(31, 44, 46–47), **44**; 'Phrygian' 20, **E2**, **E3**(29, 42–43), 42; *pilos* (later *kōnos*) **3**, **18**, **19**, **20**, 20, **21**, **F3**(30, 43–44)
hipparchos (cavalry commander) 10
historical background 3–6; Roman wars 5–6
historical sources 6–7
hypaspistai 8, 22–23
hypēretai ('sergeant-majors') 23, 24

infantry 13, 15–24, 33–37
c.280 BC **F**(30, 43–44)
cuirasses 20–21, **21**
epheboi 22
guard **E**(29, 42–43)
gymnasiarchos 22
helmets *see* helmets, infantry
organization 22–24; *chiliarchia* ('thousand') 24, **E**(29, 42–43); *lochos* (file) 22, 23; *speirarchai* (subdivision of phalanx) 23–24; *stratēgiai* (grouping at higher level) 24; *tetrarchia* (unit) 22, 23
pay 33
phalanx regiments 24, 33–37; *agēma* ('vanguard' elite) 34–35; *chalkaspides* 18, **19**, 22, **G**(31, 44, 46–47), 35–36, **37**; *leukaspides* ('white shields') 36–37; *peltastai* (elite regiment) **F2**(30, 43–44), 33, 34, 35
recruitment 21–22
shields *see* shields, infantry
weapons *see* weapons
infantrymen of the guard **E**(29, 42–43)
Ipsos, battle of (301) 3

Kallikles **G2**(31, 44, 46–47), **44**
Kallinikos, battle of (171) 12, 13
Kassandros, King, son of Antipatros 3, 4, 8, 10
kausiai (berets) 8–9, **10**, **B1**, **B3**(26, 41), **C2**(27, 41–42), **D**(28, 42)
Kleomenes III of Sparta 5, 17, 37
Kynoskephalai: battle of (197) 5, 6, 12, 34, 35; campaign 24

Lefkadia, tomb of Lyson and Kallikles **G**(31, 44, 46–47), **44**, **47**
Lysimacheia, battle of (277) 4, **18**
Lysimachos 3, 4
Lyson **G1**(31, 44, 46–47), **44**, 47

Macedonian Wars: First (214–205) 5; Second (200–197) 5; Third (171–168) 6, 12–13; Fourth (150–148) 6
Macedonicus 6
Menelaus, King **43**, 44
Menon of Antigoneia 13

Metellus, Quintus Caecilius 6
Midon of Beroea 13
Nikanor, son of Herakleides **11**
Nikolaos, son of Hadymos **3**

Oeaneum, siege of (169) 34
Olympias (Alexander's mother) 3

Pages, Royal (*basilikoi paides*) 8, **9**, **C1**(27, 41–42), 34, **38**
Peloponnese 4, 5
Perikeiromenē (play) 24
Perseus, King 4, 6, **7**, 7, 8, 12, 13, 34, 35, 37
'Petsas Tomb' **12**
Philip II, King 10
Philip III Arrhidaios, King 3, 4
Philip IV, King 4
Philip V, King 4, 5, **6**, 6, 8, 10, 12, **19**, 19, 22, **H1**(32, 47), 33, 34, 35, 37, **46**
Philip VI Andriskos, King 4, 6, **8**
Pompeii, 'House of the Menander' **43**, 43, **44**
Ptolemy 3, 4
Pydna, battle of (168) 6, **13**, 17, 33, 34, 36–37, 43, 44
Pydna, battle of (148) 6
Pyrrhos 4

Rhodes, siege of (305) 3
Roman wars 5–6
rulers of Macedonia 4

Salamis, sea battle of (306) 3, 44
Seleukos 3, 4
Sellasia: battle of (222) 5, 12, 34, 35, **37**, 37; campaign 12
shields 3, 5, **F3**(30, 43–44)
cavalry 9, **13**, **C**(27, 41–42), **F1**(30, 43–44), **G1**(31, 44, 46–47), **44**
infantry 17–20, **19**, **23**, **E**(29, 42–43), **F2**(30, 43–44), **G2**(31, 44, 46–47), **37**, **44**; *peltai* 18; Staro Bonče 18, **19**; *strovilos* symbol 5, 19, **22**
Social War (220–217) 5, 11, 22, 34, 35
Sparta 5
Stratonikos, son of Straton **38**, 41

Thalna, P. Juventius 6
Theophrastus 15
Thessalians 12, **D**(28, 42)
Thessaly 4, 5, 6
trees: ash 16; cornel-wood (wild cherry) **13**, **15**, 15–16
Troy, fall of **43**
tunics: cavalry **A**(25, 41), **B**(26, 41), **C**(27, 41–42), **D**(28, 42); infantry **E**(29, 42–43), **F2**(30, 43–44); Persian-style long-sleeved 3

weapons
ballistae (stone-throwers) 37
catapults (dart-throwers) 37
daggers **F2**(30, 43–44), 33
spears **5**, **13**; cavalry (*xysta*) 9, **A2**(25, 41), **B**(26, 41), **C2**(27, 41–42), **D**(28, 42); *pelta* 33; *sarisai* 13, 15–17, **16**, **E**(29, 42–43), 33; spear-butt **15**
swords **B3**(26, 41), **G2**(31, 44, 46–47), **44**

Zoilos, son of Ischomachos **21**